Baking

Published in 2011 by Murdoch Books Pty Limited.

Murdoch Books Pty Ltd
Pier 8/9, 23 Hickson Road,
Millers Point NSW 2000
Phone: + 61 (0) 2 8220 2000
Fax: + 61 (0) 2 8220 2558
www.murdochbooks.com.au

Murdoch Books UK Limited
Erico House, 6th Floor
93–99 Upper Richmond Road
Putney, London SW15 2TG
Phone: +44 (0)20 8785 5995
Fax: +44 (0)20 8785 5985
www.murdochbooks.co.uk

Publisher: Lynn Lewis
Project Manager: Liz Malcolm
Designer: Kylie Mulquin
Editor: Justine Harding
Production: Alexandra Gonzalez

National Library of Australia Cataloguing-in-Publication:
Title: Baking.
ISBN: 978-1-74266-507-8 (pbk.)
Series: Easy eats.
Notes: Includes index.
Subjects: Baking.
Dewey Number: 641.815

Printed by Hang Tai Printing Company Limited, China.
PRINTED IN CHINA

IMPORTANT: Those who might be at risk from the effects of salmonella poisoning (the elderly, pregnant women, young children and those suffering from immune deficiency diseases) should consult their doctor with any concerns about eating raw eggs.

CONVERSION GUIDE: You may find cooking times vary depending on the oven you are using. For fan-forced ovens, as a general rule, set the oven temperature to 20°C (35°F) lower than indicated in the recipe.

Baking

more than 100
savoury dishes and
sweet treats

MURDOCH BOOKS

MILK
MILK

Contents

Savoury

Pies and pastries with their golden crust are satisfying to make and even more of a pleasure to eat.

CHEDDAR SODA BREAD WITH PICKLED CAULIFLOWER

preparation time 30 minutes
cooking time 50 minutes
serves 6

CHEDDAR SODA BREAD

200 g (7 oz/1⅓ cups) plain (all-purpose) flour
200 g (7 oz/1⅓ cups) wholemeal (whole-wheat) plain (all-purpose) flour
2 teaspoons baking powder
1 teaspoon bicarbonate of soda (baking soda)
2 teaspoons sea salt
2½ tablespoons caster (superfine) sugar
60 g (2¼ oz) butter, chopped
250 g (9 oz/2 cups) grated cheddar cheese
350 ml (12 fl oz) buttermilk, approximately

PICKLED CAULIFLOWER

2½ tablespoons vegetable oil
2 brown onions, cut into 2 cm (¾ inch) chunks
2 teaspoons yellow mustard seeds
1 teaspoon cumin seeds
1 teaspoon ground turmeric
1 teaspoon chilli flakes
1 cauliflower (about 700 g/1 lb 9 oz), trimmed and cut into small florets
250 ml (9 fl oz/1 cup) white vinegar
110 g (3¾ oz/½ cup) caster (superfine) sugar
200 g (7 oz) green beans, trimmed and cut into short lengths

- Preheat the oven to 180°C (350°F/Gas 4).

- To make the cheddar soda bread, lightly grease and flour a baking tray. Sift together the flours, baking powder, bicarbonate of soda and salt into a large bowl, returning any wholemeal flour solids to the mixture. Stir in the sugar, then rub in the butter until evenly incorporated. Stir in the cheddar, then pour in the buttermilk and stir with a flat-bladed knife until a soft dough forms; it might be necessary to add a little more buttermilk to bring the mixture together. Turn out onto a floured surface and briefly knead until smooth. Shape into a round loaf about 20 cm (8 inches) in diameter. Using a sharp knife, slash a deep cross in the top of the loaf.

- Place the loaf on the prepared tray and bake for 50 minutes, or until it is cooked through and crusty; the loaf should sound hollow when tapped on the base. Transfer to a wire rack to cool.

- While the bread is baking, prepare the pickled cauliflower. Heat the oil in a large saucepan over medium heat. Cook the onion, stirring, for 2–3 minutes, or until softened slightly. Add the spices and cook for 2 minutes, or until aromatic, stirring often. Add the cauliflower and toss to coat well, then add the vinegar, sugar and 125 ml (4 fl oz/½ cup) water, stirring to dissolve the sugar. Bring to a simmer, cover and cook over medium heat for 2 minutes. Add the beans and cook, covered, for a final 2 minutes. Remove the pan from the heat. Keeping the lid on, set aside until the mixture is cool.

- Slice the soda bread using a serrated knife. Serve spread with butter and the pickled cauliflower.

CHEESE SCONES

preparation time 15 minutes
cooking time 15 minutes
makes 12

250 g (9 oz/2 cups) self-raising flour
1 teaspoon baking powder
½ teaspoon dry mustard
30 g (1 oz) butter, chilled and cubed
25 g (1 oz/¼ cup) freshly grated parmesan cheese
90 g (3¼ oz/¾ cup) finely grated cheddar cheese
250 ml (9 fl oz/1 cup) milk

• Preheat the oven to 220°C (425°F/Gas 7). Lightly grease a baking tray or line with baking paper. Sift the flour, baking powder, mustard and a pinch of salt into a bowl. Using your fingertips, rub in the butter until the mixture resembles fine breadcrumbs. Stir in the grated parmesan and 60 g (2¼ oz/½ cup) of the cheddar, making sure they don't clump together. Make a well in the centre.

• Add almost all the milk and mix with a flat-bladed knife, using a cutting action, until the dough comes together in clumps. Use the remaining milk if necessary. With floured hands, gently gather the dough together, lift out onto a lightly floured surface and pat it into a smooth ball. Do not knead or the scones will be tough.

• Pat the dough out to 2 cm (¾ inch) thick. Using a floured 5 cm (2 inch) biscuit (cookie) cutter, cut into rounds. Gather the trimmings and, without over-handling, press out as before and cut more rounds. Place the rounds close together on the tray and sprinkle with the remaining cheese. Bake for 12–15 minutes, or until risen and golden brown. Serve the scones warm or at room temperature.

SPICY VEGETABLE MUFFINS

preparation time 20 minutes
cooking time 25 minutes
makes 12

250 g (9 oz/2 cups) self-raising flour
3 teaspoons curry powder
80 g (2¾ oz/½ cup) grated carrot
60 g (2¼ oz/½ cup) grated orange sweet potato
125 g (4½ oz/1 cup) grated cheddar cheese
90 g (3¼ oz) butter, melted
1 egg, lightly beaten
185 ml (6 fl oz/¾ cup) milk

- Preheat the oven to 180°C (350°F/Gas 4). Lightly grease a 12-hole standard muffin tin, or line the muffin tin with paper cases. Sift the flour, curry powder and some salt and pepper into a bowl. Add the carrot, sweet potato and cheese and mix through with your fingertips until the ingredients are evenly combined. Make a well in the centre.

- Combine the butter, egg and milk and add to the flour mixture all at once. Using a wooden spoon, stir until the ingredients are just combined. Do not overmix — the batter will still be slightly lumpy.

- Divide the mixture evenly among the holes — fill each hole about three-quarters full. Bake for 20–25 minutes, or until golden and a skewer inserted into the centre of a muffin comes out clean. Leave in the tin for a couple of minutes. Gently loosen each muffin with a flat-bladed knife before turning out onto a wire rack. Serve warm or at room temperature.

SOURDOUGH BREAD

preparation time 30 minutes plus proving
cooking time 40 minutes
makes 2 loaves

STARTER
125 g (4½ oz/1 cup) white strong flour
2 teaspoons fresh yeast

SPONGE
125 g (4½ oz/1 cup) white strong flour

DOUGH
375 g (13 oz/3 cups) white strong flour
2 teaspoons fresh yeast

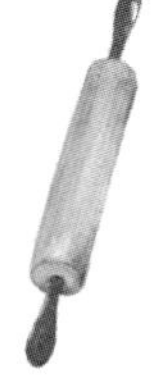

• To make the starter, sift the flour into a bowl and make a well in the centre. Cream the yeast and 250 ml (9 fl oz/1 cup) warm water together, pour into the flour and gradually draw the flour into the centre to form a thick smooth paste. Cover with plastic wrap or a damp tea towel (dish towel) and leave at room temperature for 24 hours. The starter will begin to ferment and bubble.

• To make the sponge, stir the flour into the starter mixture and gradually whisk in 125 ml (4 fl oz/½ cup) warm water to form a smooth mixture. Cover with plastic wrap and leave for 24 hours.

• To make the dough, sift the flour and 1 teaspoon salt into a large bowl and make a well in the centre. Cream the yeast and 80 ml (2½ fl oz/⅓ cup) warm water together and add to the dry ingredients with the starter and sponge mixture. Gradually incorporate the flour into the well. Turn the dough onto a lightly floured surface and knead for 10 minutes, or until smooth and elastic, incorporating extra flour if needed.

• Place the dough in a lightly oiled bowl, cover with plastic wrap or a damp tea towel (dish towel) and place in a warm place for 1 hour, or until doubled in size. Lightly grease two baking trays and dust lightly with flour. Punch the dough down and turn onto the work surface. Knead for 1 minute, or until smooth. Divide into two equal portions and shape each portion into a 20 cm (8 inch) round. Using a sharp knife, score diagonal cuts 1 cm (½ inch) deep along the loaves.

• Place the loaves on the trays and cover with plastic wrap or a damp tea towel. Leave in a warm place for 45 minutes, or until doubled in size. Preheat the oven to 190°C (375°F/Gas 5).

• Bake for 35–40 minutes, changing the breads around halfway through. Bake until the bread is golden and crusty and sounds hollow when tapped. Cool on a wire rack before cutting.

OLIVE BREAD

preparation time 30 minutes plus proving
cooking time 35 minutes
makes 1 loaf

375 g (13 oz/3 cups) plain (all-purpose) flour
2 teaspoons dried yeast
2 teaspoons sugar
2 tablespoons olive oil
110 g (3¾ oz/⅔ cup) pitted and halved Kalamata olives
2 teaspoons plain (all-purpose) flour, extra, to coat
1 small oregano sprig, leaves removed and torn into small pieces (optional)
olive oil, to glaze

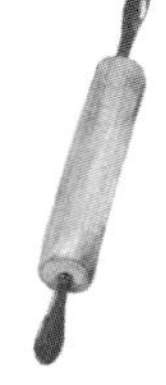

• Put one-third of the flour in a large bowl and stir in 1 teaspoon salt. Put the yeast, sugar and 250 ml (9 fl oz/1 cup) warm water in a small bowl and stir well. Leave the mixture in a warm, draught-free place for 10 minutes, or until bubbles appear on the surface. The mixture should appear frothy and slightly increased in volume. If your yeast doesn't foam, it is dead, so you will have to discard it and start again.

• Add the yeast mixture to the flour mixture and stir to make a thin, lumpy paste. Cover with a tea towel (dish towel) and set aside in a warm, draught-free place for 45 minutes, or until doubled in size.

• Stir in the remaining flour and the oil and 125 ml (4 fl oz/½ cup) warm water. Mix with a wooden spoon until a rough dough forms. Transfer to a lightly floured work surface and knead for 10–12 minutes, incorporating as little extra flour as possible to keep the dough soft and moist, but not sticky. Form into a ball. Oil a clean large bowl and roll the dough around in it to coat in the oil. Cut a cross on top, cover the bowl with a tea towel and set aside in a warm place for 1 hour, or until doubled in size.

- Lightly grease a baking tray and dust with flour. Punch down the dough on a lightly floured surface. Roll out to 1 x 25 x 30 cm (½ x 10 x 12 inches). Squeeze any excess liquid from the olives and toss to coat in the extra flour. Scatter over the dough and top with the oregano. Roll up tightly lengthways, pressing firmly to expel any air pockets as you roll. Press the ends together to form an oval loaf 25 cm (10 inches) long. Transfer to the prepared tray, join side down. Make three shallow diagonal slashes across the top. Slide the tray into a large plastic bag and leave in a warm place for 45 minutes, or until doubled in bulk.

- Preheat the oven to 220°C (425°F/Gas 7). Brush the top of the loaf with oil and bake for 30 minutes. Reduce the heat to 180°C (350°F/Gas 4) and bake for another 5 minutes. Cool on a wire rack. Serve warm or cold.

Note *Instead of the oregano you can use 2 teaspoons finely chopped rosemary. Fold it through the dough and sprinkle whole leaves on the top after brushing with olive oil.*

PUMPKIN AND SAGE SCONES

preparation time 10 minutes
cooking time 20 minutes
makes 8

250 g (9 oz/2 cups) self-raising flour
250 g (9 oz/1 cup) cooked and puréed pumpkin (winter squash)
20 g (¾ oz) butter
1 tablespoon chopped sage
milk

• Preheat the oven to 180°C (350°F/Gas 4). Lightly grease a baking tray or line with baking paper. Sift the flour into a bowl with a pinch of salt. Using your fingertips, rub the pumpkin and butter into the flour and then add the sage.

• Bring the mixture together with a little milk and turn it out onto the tray. Shape the mixture into a round and roll it out to about 3 cm (1¼ inches) thick. Gently mark or cut the scone into eight segments and bake for 15–20 minutes, or until lightly browned and cooked through.

CHILLI POLENTA CAKE

preparation time 25 minutes
cooking time 30 minutes
makes one 20 cm (8 inch) cake

165 g (5¾ oz/1⅓ cups) plain (all-purpose) flour
1½ teaspoons baking powder
185 g (6½ oz/1¼ cups) polenta
125 g (4½ oz/1 cup) grated cheddar cheese
250 g (9 oz/1 cup) plain yoghurt
125 ml (4 fl oz/½ cup) milk
2 eggs
80 g (2¾ oz/½ cup) chopped red capsicum (pepper)
2 teaspoons chopped chilli
60 g (2¼ oz) unsalted butter

• Preheat the oven to 200°C (400°F/Gas 6). Sift the flour, baking powder and 1 teaspoon salt into a large bowl. Mix in the polenta and cheese.

• In a separate bowl, whisk together the plain yoghurt, milk, eggs, red capsicum and chilli.

• Heat a 20 cm (8 inch) ovenproof frying pan and melt the butter. Stir the butter into the yoghurt mixture, then pour all the liquid ingredients into the dry ingredients. Mix well.

• Pour the batter into the frying pan. Cook in the oven for 25–30 minutes, or until a skewer inserted in the centre comes out clean.

HAM, CHEESE AND ONION QUICKBREAD

preparation time 25 minutes
cooking time 1 hour 5 minutes
makes 1 loaf

1 tablespoon oil
3 onions, thinly sliced into rings
2 teaspoons soft brown sugar
200 g (7 oz) sliced ham, finely chopped
375 g (13 oz/3 cups) self-raising flour
100 g (3½ oz) chilled butter
90 g (3¼ oz/¾ cup) grated cheddar cheese
125 ml (4 fl oz/½ cup) milk

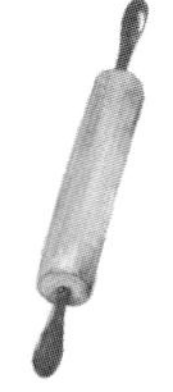

• Heat half of the oil in a large, heavy-based frying pan. Add the onion and cook over medium heat for 10 minutes, stirring occasionally. Add the sugar and continue to cook for 10–15 minutes, or until the onion is golden brown. Set aside to cool.

• Heat the remaining oil in a small frying pan, add the ham and cook over moderately high heat until golden brown. Drain on crumpled paper towel and add to the onion. Allow to cool slightly.

• Preheat the oven to 210°C (415°F/Gas 6–7). Lightly grease a baking tray. Sift the flour into a large bowl and rub in the butter with your fingertips until the mixture resembles fine breadcrumbs.

• Add three-quarters of the onion mixture and 60 g (2¼ oz/½ cup) of the cheddar to the flour and mix well. Make a well in the centre and add the milk and about 125 ml (4 fl oz/½ cup) of water (add enough to bring the dough together). Mix with a flat-bladed knife, using a cutting action, until the mixture forms a soft dough. Gently gather together into a ball.

• Lay the dough on the tray and press out to form a 22 cm (8½ inch) circle. Using a sharp knife, mark the dough into quarters, cutting two-thirds of the way through. Sprinkle with the rest of the onion mixture and the remaining cheddar. Bake for 15 minutes, then reduce the oven to 180°C (350°F/Gas 4). Cover the top loosely with foil if it starts getting too brown. Bake for another 20 minutes, or until the base sounds hollow when tapped.

FENNEL AND FETA ROLLS

preparation time 30 minutes
cooking time 40 minutes
serves 4

1 tablespoon extra virgin olive oil
1 rosemary sprig
1 fennel bulb (about 350 g/12 oz), trimmed and cut into 1 cm (½ inch) pieces
1 large red onion, cut into 1 cm (½ inch) pieces
185 ml (6 fl oz/¾ cup) chicken stock
75 g (2¾ oz/½ cup) crumbled feta cheese
1½ tablespoons chopped parsley
4 sheets filo pastry
50 g (1¾ oz) butter, melted
taramasalata, to serve (available from supermarkets and delis)

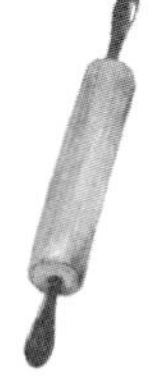

• Heat the oil in a saucepan over medium heat. Add the rosemary, fennel and onion and stir to coat in the oil. Reduce the heat to low, cover and cook, stirring occasionally, for 10 minutes, until the vegetables begin to soften. Add the stock, bring to the boil over medium heat, cover, reduce the heat to low and cook for 10–15 minutes, or until the vegetables are very soft and the liquid is absorbed. Cook, uncovered, to evaporate any excess liquid if necessary. Season to taste, then cool. Remove the rosemary, then stir in the feta and parsley.

• Preheat the oven to 190°C (375°F/Gas 5). Lay one sheet of filo on a clean work surface, keeping the remaining sheets covered to prevent them drying out. Brush with melted butter, then lay another sheet of filo on top. Cut the pastry in half lengthways, then in half widthways to give four pieces. Lightly brush each piece with butter. Divide the filling into eight portions, then place one portion along a short side of one of the pieces of filo. Fold the sides of the pastry over each end of the filling, then roll the pastry up to form a log. Repeat with the remaining filo, butter and filling, then transfer the rolls to a baking tray. Bake for 12–15 minutes or until golden and crisp. Serve the rolls with a spoonful of taramasalata on the side.

GOAT'S CHEESE GALETTE

preparation time 20 minutes
cooking time 1 hour 15 minutes
serves 6

PASTRY
125 g (4½ oz/1 cup) plain (all-purpose) flour
60 ml (2 fl oz/¼ cup) olive oil

FILLING
1 tablespoon olive oil
2 onions, thinly sliced
1 teaspoon thyme
125 g (4½ oz) ricotta cheese
100 g (3½ oz) goat's cheese
2 tablespoons pitted niçoise olives
1 egg, beaten
60 ml (2 fl oz/¼ cup) cream

• To make the pastry, sift the flour and a pinch of salt into a bowl and make a well in the centre. Add the oil and mix with a flat-bladed knife until crumbly. Gradually add 60–80 ml (2–2½ fl oz/¼–⅓ cup) water until the mixture comes together. Remove and pat together to form a disc. Refrigerate for 30 minutes.

• Meanwhile, to make the filling, heat the oil in a frying pan. Add the onion, cover and cook for 30 minutes. Season and stir in half the thyme. Cool.

• Preheat the oven to 180°C (350°F/Gas 4). Lightly flour the workbench and roll out the pastry to a 30 cm (12 inch) circle, then place on a heated baking tray. Spread the onion over the pastry, leaving a 2 cm (¾ inch) border. Sprinkle the ricotta and goat's cheese over the onion. Put the olives over the cheeses, then sprinkle with the remaining thyme. Fold the pastry border in to the edge of the filling, pleating as you go.

• Combine the egg and cream, then pour over the filling. Bake in the lower half of the oven for 45 minutes, or until the pastry is golden.

TOMATO-FETA TARTS WITH LEMON AND OREGANO

preparation time 30 minutes plus 30 minutes chilling
cooking time 35 minutes
serves 6

125 g (4½ oz) chilled butter, cubed
250 g (9 oz/1⅔ cups) plain (all-purpose) flour, sifted, plus extra, for dusting
1 egg, lightly beaten
2 teaspoons finely grated lemon rind
800 g (1 lb 12 oz) grape tomatoes (400 g/14 oz each yellow and red)
2 tablespoons olive oil
2 garlic cloves, thinly sliced
1 tablespoon finely chopped oregano leaves, plus whole leaves, to serve
1 tablespoon balsamic vinegar
60 g (2¼ oz) feta cheese, crumbled

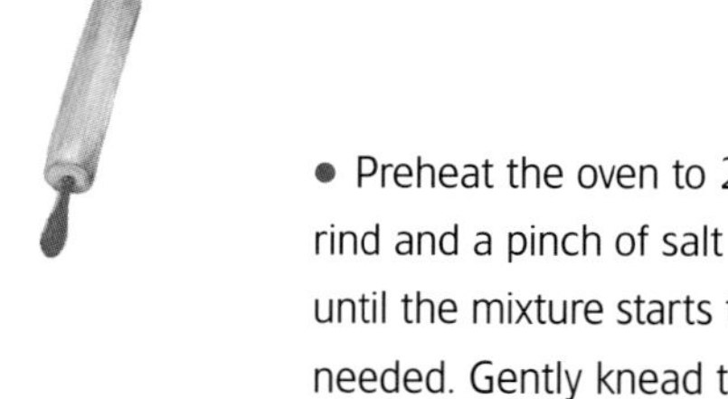

• Preheat the oven to 200°C (400°F/Gas 6). Place the butter, flour, egg, lemon rind and a pinch of salt into a food processor bowl. Process for 30 seconds, or until the mixture starts to clump together. Add 1–2 teaspoons of chilled water if needed. Gently knead together on a floured board, then divide the mixture into six portions. (Alternatively, put the butter, flour and a pinch of salt in a bowl and rub the butter into the flour until the mixture resembles coarse breadcrumbs. Mix in the egg and lemon rind until the mixture starts to clump together, then gently knead on a floured board, and divide into six portions.) Roll each portion into a flattened disc, place on a tray, cover and chill for 30 minutes.

• Meanwhile, cut the tomatoes in half and place in a single layer on a baking tray. Drizzle with the oil, then scatter over the garlic and season with sea salt and freshly ground black pepper. Bake for 12–15 minutes or until softened. Cool the tomatoes slightly, then combine in a bowl with the chopped oregano and vinegar, and stir gently. Set aside.

• Reduce the oven temperature to 180°C (350°F/Gas 4) and lightly grease six 10 cm (4 inch) tartlet tins with removable bases. Roll out each portion of pastry between two sheets of baking paper until about 3 mm (1/8 inch) thick and large enough to line the tins. Press the pastry into the tins, cutting off any excess. Prick the bases with a fork. Line the pastry with baking paper and fill with rice or baking beads. Bake for 10 minutes, then remove the rice or beads, and cook for a further 8–10 minutes or until pastry is light golden. Cool.

• To serve, divide the tomato filling among the pastry cases, sprinkle the feta over the top, scatter with oregano leaves and serve immediately.

SPINACH PIE

preparation time 35 minutes
cooking time 40 minutes
serves 6–8

500 g (1 lb 2 oz) English spinach
1 tablespoon oil
6 spring onions (scallions), finely chopped
125 g (4½ oz) feta cheese, crumbled
90 g (3¼ oz/¾ cup) grated cheddar cheese
5 eggs, lightly beaten
16 sheets filo pastry
80 ml (2½ fl oz/⅓ cup) olive oil
1 egg, extra, lightly beaten, to glaze
1 tablespoon poppy seeds or sesame seeds

• Preheat the oven to 210°C (415°F/Gas 6–7) and brush a 25 x 30 cm (10 x 12 inch) ovenproof dish with oil. Wash the spinach thoroughly and shred finely. Put in a large saucepan with just the water that is clinging to the leaves. Cook, covered, over low heat for 2 minutes, or until just wilted. Cool, wring out any excess water and spread out the strands.

• Heat the oil in a small frying pan and cook the spring onion for 3 minutes, or until soft. Transfer to a large bowl and add the spinach, cheeses and eggs, then season. Stir until the cheeses are distributed evenly. Place one sheet of pastry in the dish, letting the edges overhang. Cover the remaining pastry with a clean, damp tea towel (dish towel) to prevent it drying out. Brush the pastry in the dish with oil. Repeat with another seven layers of pastry, lightly brushing each with oil.

• Spread the filling over the pastry, then fold in the edges. Lightly brush each remaining sheet of pastry with oil and place on top of the pie. Tuck the edges down the sides, brush the top with egg and sprinkle with poppy seeds. Bake for 35–40 minutes, or until the pastry is golden. Serve immediately.

CHERRY TOMATO AND PESTO TART

preparation time 15 minutes
cooking time 10 minutes
serves 4

500 g (1 lb 2 oz) block puff pastry, thawed
125 g (4½ oz/½ cup) ready-made pesto
375 g (13 oz) cherry tomatoes
2 spring onions (scallions), finely sliced
extra virgin olive oil, to drizzle
spring onion (scallion) slices, to garnish

- Divide the pastry into two portions and roll each portion between two sheets of baking paper. If making four tartlets, cut out two 12 cm (4½ inch) circles of pastry from each portion, or for two long tartlets roll each portion of pastry into a rectangle 12 x 25 cm (4½ x 10 inches).

- Preheat the oven to 200°C (400°F/Gas 6). Spread the pesto over the pastry, leaving a 1.5 cm (⅝ inch) border. Top with the cherry tomatoes and finely sliced spring onion. Season and bake for 10 minutes, or until golden. Drizzle with extra virgin olive oil and garnish with the spring onion slices. Serve warm or hot.

POTATO PIES

preparation time 25 minutes
cooking time 1 hour 5 minutes
makes 6

- 1 kg (2 lb 4 oz) all-purpose potatoes, chopped
- 1 tablespoon oil
- 1 onion, finely chopped
- 1 garlic clove, crushed
- 500 g (1 lb 2 oz) minced (ground) beef
- 2 tablespoons plain (all-purpose) flour
- 500 ml (17 fl oz/2 cups) beef stock
- 2 tablespoons tomato paste (concentrated purée)
- 1 tablespoon worcestershire sauce
- 500 g (1 lb 2 oz) shortcrust (pie) pastry
- 50 g (1¾ oz) butter, softened
- 60 ml (2 fl oz/¼ cup) milk

• Steam or boil the potatoes for 10 minutes, or until tender (pierce with the point of a small sharp knife and if the potato comes away easily it is ready). Drain thoroughly, then mash.

• Preheat the oven to 210°C (415°F/Gas 6–7). Heat the oil in a frying pan, add the onion and cook for 5 minutes, or until soft. Add the garlic and cook for 1 minute. Add the beef and cook over medium heat for 5 minutes, until browned, breaking up any lumps with a fork.

• Sprinkle the flour over the meat and stir to combine. Add the stock, tomato paste, worcestershire sauce and some salt and pepper to the pan and stir for 2 minutes. Bring to the boil, reduce the heat slightly and simmer for 5 minutes, or until the mixture has reduced and thickened. Cool completely.

• Lightly grease six 11 cm (4 ¼ inch) pie tins. Roll out the pastry between two sheets of baking paper and, using a plate as a guide, cut the pastry into 15 cm (6 inch) circles and line the pie tins. Cut baking paper to cover each tin, spread baking beads or uncooked rice over the paper and bake for 7 minutes. Remove the paper and beads or rice and cook the pastry for another 5 minutes. Allow to cool.

• Divide the meat filling among the pastry cases. Stir the butter and milk into the mashed potato and pipe or spread all over the top of the meat filling. Bake for 20 minutes, or until the potato is lightly golden.

FETA AND OLIVE HERB PIE

preparation time 40 minutes plus proving
cooking time 45 minutes
serves 4–6

PASTRY

1 teaspoon sugar
2 teaspoons dried yeast
1 tablespoon olive oil
60 g (2¼ oz/½ cup) plain (all-purpose) flour
125 g (4½ oz/1 cup) self-raising flour

FILLING

1 tablespoon olive oil
1 onion, sliced
1 teaspoon sugar
15 g (½ oz) flat-leaf (Italian) parsley, chopped
1 rosemary sprig, chopped
3 thyme sprigs, chopped
5 basil leaves, torn
40 g (1½ oz/¼ cup) pine nuts, toasted (see Note)
1 garlic clove, crushed
175 g (6 oz) feta cheese, crumbled
30 g (1 oz) pitted olives, chopped

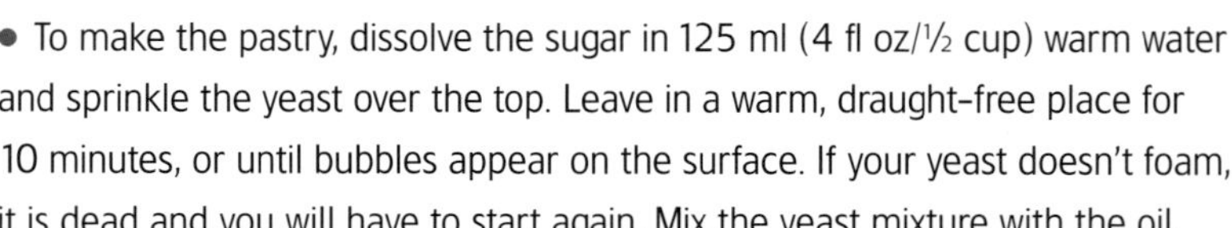

• To make the pastry, dissolve the sugar in 125 ml (4 fl oz/½ cup) warm water and sprinkle the yeast over the top. Leave in a warm, draught-free place for 10 minutes, or until bubbles appear on the surface. If your yeast doesn't foam, it is dead and you will have to start again. Mix the yeast mixture with the oil.

• Sift the flours and ½ teaspoon salt into a large bowl. Make a well in the centre and pour in the yeast mixture. Mix well and knead on a lightly floured board until smooth. Cut the dough in half, then roll each half into a 20 cm (8 inch) circle. Place one circle on a lightly greased baking tray, the other on a baking tray covered with baking paper. Cover the circles with a cloth and put in a warm place for 10–15 minutes, or until doubled in size. Preheat the oven to 200°C (400°F/Gas 6).

- To make the filling, heat the oil in a frying pan and cook the onion for 10 minutes, or until golden brown. Sprinkle with the sugar and cook for a further 5 minutes, or until caramelised. Transfer to a bowl and mix with the herbs, pine nuts, garlic, feta and olives.

- Spread the filling over the pastry on the greased tray. Brush the edge with water and put the second pastry circle on top, using the paper to help lift it over. Press the edges together to seal and pinch together to form a pattern. Cut a few slits in the top of the pastry. Bake for 30–35 minutes, or until crisp and golden brown. Serve warm, cut into wedges.

Note *To toast pine nuts, you can dry-fry them in a frying pan, stirring and watching them constantly so they don't burn.*

HARVEST PIE

preparation time 40 minutes
cooking time 1 hour
serves 6

PASTRY
250 g (9 oz/2 cups) plain (all-purpose) flour
125 g (4½ oz) butter, chopped
60 ml (2 fl oz/¼ cup) iced water

FILLING
1 tablespoon oil
1 onion, finely chopped
1 small red capsicum (pepper), seeded, membrane removed and chopped
1 small green capsicum (pepper), seeded, membrane removed and chopped

150 g (5½ oz) pumpkin (winter squash), chopped
1 small potato, chopped
100 g (3½ oz) broccoli, cut into small florets
1 carrot, chopped
50 g (1¾ oz) butter
30 g (1 oz/¼ cup) plain (all-purpose) flour, extra
250 ml (9 fl oz/1 cup) milk
2 egg yolks
60 g (2¼ oz/½ cup) grated cheddar cheese
1 egg, lightly beaten, to glaze

- Preheat the oven to 180°C (350°F/Gas 4).

- To make the pastry, sift the flour into a large bowl. Using your fingertips, rub in the butter until the mixture resembles fine breadcrumbs. Add almost all the water and mix with a flat-bladed knife, using a cutting action until the mixture forms a firm dough, adding more water if necessary. Turn onto a lightly floured work surface and press together until smooth.

- Divide the dough in half, roll out one portion and line a deep 21 cm (8¼ inch) fluted flan (tart) tin. Refrigerate for 20 minutes. Roll the remaining pastry out to a 25 cm (10 inch) diameter circle. Cut into strips and lay half of them on a sheet of baking paper, leaving a 1 cm (½ inch) gap between each strip. Interweave the remaining strips to form a lattice pattern. Cover with plastic wrap and refrigerate, keeping flat, until firm.

- Cut a sheet of baking paper to cover the pastry-lined tin. Spread a layer of baking beads or uncooked rice over the paper. Bake for 10 minutes, remove from the oven and discard the paper and beads. Bake for another 10 minutes, or until lightly golden. Allow to cool.

- To make the filling, heat the oil in a frying pan. Add the onion and cook for 2 minutes, or until soft. Add the capsicum and cook, stirring, for 3 minutes. Steam or boil the remaining vegetables until just tender. Drain and cool. Mix the onion, capsicum and other vegetables in a large bowl.

- Heat the butter in a small saucepan. Add the flour and cook, stirring, for 2 minutes. Add the milk gradually, stirring until smooth between each addition. Stir constantly over medium heat until the mixture boils and thickens. Boil for 1 minute and then remove from the heat. Add the egg yolks and cheese and stir until smooth. Pour the sauce over the vegetables and stir to combine.

- Pour the mixture into the pastry case and brush the edges with egg. Using the baking paper to lift, invert the pastry lattice over the vegetables. Trim the pastry edges and brush with a little beaten egg, sealing it to the cooked pastry. Brush the top with egg and bake for 30 minutes, or until golden brown.

CORN AND RED CAPSICUM QUICHES

preparation time 30 minutes
cooking time 20 minutes
makes 24

2 sheets ready-rolled shortcrust (pie) pastry
135 g (4¾ oz) tinned corn kernels, drained
40 g (1½ oz/⅓ cup) grated cheddar cheese
½ red capsicum (pepper), seeded, membrane removed and finely chopped
2 eggs
170 ml (5½ fl oz/⅔ cup) cream
2 teaspoons dijon mustard
dash Tabasco sauce

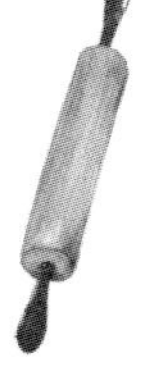

• Preheat the oven to 200°C (400°F/Gas 6). Grease two shallow 12-hole patty pans or mini muffin tins. Lay the pastry on a lightly floured work surface and cut 12 rounds from each sheet with an 8 cm (3¼ inch) cutter. Line the tins with the pastry circles.

• Mix the corn kernels with the cheddar and red capsicum. Beat the eggs, cream, mustard and Tabasco sauce. Divide the corn mixture among the pastry cases and top with the egg mixture until almost full. Bake for 15–20 minutes, or until puffed and golden. Remove the warm quiches from the tins and cool on wire racks.

TOMATO AND BOCCONCINI FLAN

preparation time 30 minutes
cooking time 50 minutes
serves 6

185 g (6½ oz/1½ cups) plain (all-purpose) flour
100 g (3½ oz) butter, chopped
1 egg
2 tablespoons cold water
5–6 roma (plum) tomatoes
1 tablespoon olive oil
8 bocconcini (fresh baby mozzarella cheese), about 220 g/7¾ oz, sliced
6 spring onions (scallions), chopped
2 tablespoons chopped rosemary

• Combine the flour and butter in a food processor. Process for 10 seconds, or until fine and crumbly. Combine the egg and water in a small bowl. With the motor running, gradually add to the flour mixture and process until the mixture just comes together. Turn out onto a lightly floured surface and knead to form a smooth dough. Refrigerate, covered with plastic wrap, for 20 minutes.

• Preheat the oven to 210°C (415°F/Gas 6–7). Roll out the pastry on a floured surface to fit a 23 cm (9 inch) round, loose-based flan (tart) tin. Ease into the tin and trim the edges. Cover the pastry with a sheet of baking paper. Spread a layer of baking beads or uncooked rice over the paper. Bake for 15 minutes, then remove the paper and beads and bake for another 10 minutes, until the pastry is lightly golden, then cool. Reduce the oven to 180°C (350°F/Gas 4).

• Cut the tomatoes in half, sprinkle with salt and drizzle with the oil. Place in an ovenproof dish, cut side up, and bake for 15 minutes.

• Arrange the tomatoes, cut side up, over the pastry. Place the bocconcini slices and spring onion between the tomatoes. Scatter with the rosemary and season. Bake for 10 minutes. Remove from the oven and cool for 10 minutes before serving.

COUNTRY VEGETABLE PIES

preparation time 50 minutes
cooking time 45 minutes
serves 6

PASTRY
250 g (9 oz/2 cups) plain (all-purpose) flour
125 g ($4\frac{1}{2}$ oz) butter, chilled and cubed
2 egg yolks
2–3 tablespoons iced water

FILLING
2 new potatoes, cubed
350 g (12 oz) butternut pumpkin (squash), cubed
100 g ($3\frac{1}{2}$ oz) broccoli, cut into small florets
100 g ($3\frac{1}{2}$ oz) cauliflower, cut into small florets
1 zucchini (courgette), grated
1 carrot, grated
3 spring onions (scallions), chopped
90 g ($3\frac{1}{4}$ oz/$\frac{3}{4}$ cup) grated cheddar cheese
125 g ($4\frac{1}{2}$ oz/$\frac{1}{2}$ cup) ricotta cheese
50 g ($1\frac{3}{4}$ oz/$\frac{1}{2}$ cup) grated parmesan cheese
3 tablespoons chopped flat-leaf (Italian) parsley
1 egg, lightly beaten

• To make the pastry, sift the flour into a bowl. Using your fingertips, rub in the butter until the mixture resembles fine breadcrumbs. Make a well in the centre, add the egg yolks and the iced water and mix with a flat-bladed knife, using a cutting action, until the mixture comes together in beads. Add more water if the dough is too dry. Gently gather the dough together and lift onto a lightly floured work surface. Press into a ball, cover with plastic wrap and refrigerate for at least 15 minutes.

• To make the filling, steam or boil the potato and pumpkin for 10–15 minutes, or until just tender. Drain well and put in a large bowl to cool. Gently fold in the broccoli, cauliflower, zucchini, carrot, spring onion, cheddar, ricotta, parmesan, parsley and beaten egg. Season to taste.

• Preheat the oven to 190°C (375°F/Gas 5). Grease six 10 cm (4 inch) pie tins. Divide the pastry into six and roll each portion into a rough 20 cm (8 inch) circle. Place the pastry in the tins, leaving the excess overhanging.

• Divide the filling evenly among the pastry cases. Fold over the overhanging pastry, gently folding or pleating as you go. Place on a baking tray, cover and refrigerate for 15 minutes. Bake for 25–30 minutes, until the pastry is cooked and golden brown. Serve hot.

VEGETABLE STRUDEL

preparation time 30 minutes
cooking time 35 minutes
serves 4–6

12 English spinach leaves
2 tablespoons olive oil
1 onion, finely sliced
1 red capsicum (pepper), seeded, membrane removed and cut into strips
1 green capsicum (pepper), seeded, membrane removed and cut into strips
2 zucchinis (courgettes), sliced
2 slender eggplants (aubergines), sliced
6 sheets filo pastry
40 g (1½ oz) butter, melted
20 g (¾ oz) finely sliced basil leaves
60 g (2¼ oz/½ cup) grated cheddar cheese
2 tablespoons sesame seeds

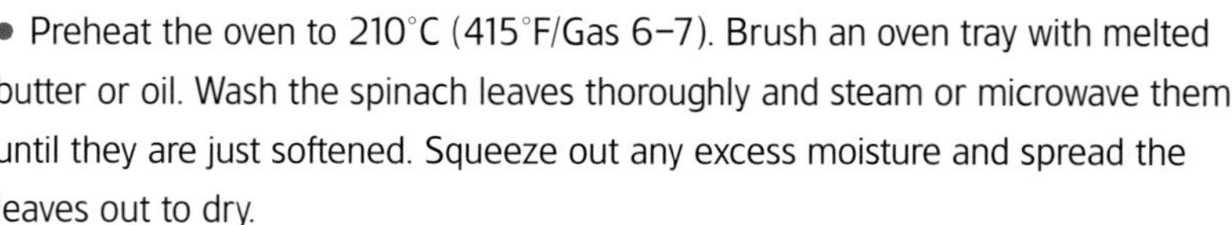

• Preheat the oven to 210°C (415°F/Gas 6–7). Brush an oven tray with melted butter or oil. Wash the spinach leaves thoroughly and steam or microwave them until they are just softened. Squeeze out any excess moisture and spread the leaves out to dry.

• Heat the oil in a frying pan, add the onion and cook over medium heat for 3 minutes. Add the capsicum, zucchini and eggplant and cook, stirring, for 5 minutes, or until the vegetables have softened. Season and then set aside to cool. Brush one sheet of filo pastry with melted butter and top with a second sheet. Repeat with the remaining pastry, brushing with butter between each layer. Place the spinach, cooled vegetable mixture, basil and cheese along one long side of the pastry, about 5 cm (2 inches) in from the edge. Fold the sides over the filling, fold the short end over and roll up tightly.

• Place the strudel, seam side down, on the prepared tray. Brush with the remaining melted butter and sprinkle with the sesame seeds. Bake for 25 minutes, or until golden brown and crisp.

SPANISH PIZZA

preparation time 30 minutes
cooking time 45 minutes
serves 4–6

BASE
2 teaspoons dried yeast
1 teaspoon caster (superfine) sugar
280 g (10 oz/2¼ cups) plain (all-purpose) flour

10 English spinach leaves, shredded
1 tablespoon olive oil
2 garlic cloves, crushed
2 onions, chopped
440 g (15½ oz) tinned tomatoes, drained and crushed
12 pitted black olives, chopped

- Preheat the oven to 210°C (415°F/Gas 6–7). Brush a 25 x 30 cm (10 x 12 inch) Swiss roll tin (jelly roll tin) with melted butter or oil.

- For the base, combine the yeast, sugar and flour in a large bowl. Gradually add 250 ml (9 fl oz/1 cup) warm water and blend until smooth. Knead the dough on a lightly floured surface until smooth and elastic. Place in a lightly oiled bowl, cover with a tea towel (dish towel) and leave to rise in a warm position for 15 minutes, or until the dough has almost doubled in size.

- To make the topping, put the spinach in a large saucepan, cover and cook over low heat for 3 minutes. Drain and cool. Squeeze out the excess moisture with your hands. Heat the oil in a frying pan and cook the garlic and onion over low heat for 5–6 minutes. Add the tomato and ¼ teaspoon ground pepper and simmer gently for 5 minutes.

- Punch the dough down and knead on a floured board for 2–3 minutes. Roll out the dough and fit it in the tin. Spread with the spinach, top with the tomato mixture and sprinkle the olives on top. Bake for 25–30 minutes. Cut into small squares or fingers. The pizza can be served hot or cold.

VEGETABLE BIRYANI WITH CUMIN PASTRY

preparation time 25 minutes
cooking time 1 hour
serves 4–6

2 tablespoons vegetable oil
2 onions, thinly sliced
2 garlic cloves, crushed
1 tablespoon finely chopped fresh ginger
1 green chilli, seeded and finely chopped
2 teaspoons garam masala
1 tablespoon curry powder
125 g (4½ oz/½ cup) Greek-style yoghurt, plus extra, to serve
60 ml (2 fl oz/¼ cup) lime juice
400 g (14 oz) pumpkin (winter squash), peeled and cut into 4 cm (1½ inch) chunks
2 potatoes, peeled and cut into 2 cm (¾ inch) chunks
½ cauliflower, cut into small florets (about 420 g/15 oz/3½ cups)
2 carrots, cut into 2 cm (¾ inch) chunks
200 g (7 oz/1 cup) basmati rice
175 g (6 oz) green beans, trimmed and cut into 4 cm (1½ inch) lengths
2 tomatoes, cut into 2 cm (¾ inch) dice
750 ml (26 fl oz/3 cups) vegetable stock
a pinch of saffron threads
40 g (1½ oz/⅓ cup) sultanas (golden raisins)
1 sheet frozen shortcrust pastry, thawed
1 egg, lightly beaten
1 teaspoon cumin seeds
coriander (cilantro) leaves, to garnish
2 tablespoons toasted cashew nuts, roughly chopped

• Preheat the oven to 180°C (350°F/Gas 4).

• Heat the oil in a 3 litre (105 fl oz/12 cup) flameproof casserole dish over medium–high heat. Add the onion and garlic and sauté for 5 minutes, or until golden. Add the ginger, chilli and spices and cook for a further 2 minutes, or until aromatic. Stir in the yoghurt and lime juice, then add the pumpkin, potato, cauliflower and carrot.

• Stir the rice through, then add the beans, tomato, stock, saffron and sultanas. Mix well and bring to the boil.

• Remove the dish from the heat, then carefully cover the top with the pastry, trimming if necessary and sealing the pastry well to ensure no steam escapes. Brush the top with beaten egg and sprinkle with the cumin seeds.

• Bake for 40 minutes, or until the pastry is golden. Remove from the oven and leave to stand for 5 minutes. Divide into serving portions and transfer to warm plates. Serve garnished with coriander, with extra yoghurt for drizzling and with chopped cashews for sprinkling over.

MEXICAN BEAN CASSEROLE ON CORNBREAD WITH AVOCADO SALSA

preparation time 30 minutes plus 10 minutes soaking
cooking time 1 hour 5 minutes
serves 4

2 tablespoons olive oil
1 brown onion, finely chopped
1 red capsicum (pepper), diced
1 green capsicum (pepper), diced
3 garlic cloves, crushed
1 teaspoon ground cumin
1 teaspoon dried oregano
440 g (15½ oz) tin kidney beans, rinsed and drained
440 g (15½ oz) tin chopped tomatoes
a pinch of cayenne pepper
½ teaspoon chilli flakes
250 ml (9 fl oz/1 cup) vegetable stock
1 small handful flat-leaf (Italian) parsley leaves, chopped
2 tablespoons lemon juice
sour cream, to serve (optional)

CORNBREAD

60 g (2¼ oz) unsalted butter, melted, plus extra, for greasing
150 g (5½ oz/1 cup) plain (all-purpose) flour
1 tablespoon baking powder
¼ teaspoon salt
1 teaspoon ground cumin
190 g (6¾ oz/1 cup) cornmeal (polenta)
60 g (2¼ oz/½ cup) finely grated cheddar cheese
2 eggs
250 ml (9 fl oz/1 cup) buttermilk

AVOCADO SALSA

2 firm, ripe avocados, coarsely diced
2½ tablespoons lemon juice
½ red onion, finely diced
2 tablespoons chopped coriander (cilantro)
¼ teaspoon Tabasco sauce, or to taste

• Heat the olive oil in a large heavy-based saucepan over medium heat. Add the onion and cook, stirring, for 5–8 minutes, or until softened. Add the capsicum and cook, stirring often, for a further 5 minutes, until the capsicum starts to soften. Stir in the garlic, cumin and oregano and cook for 1 minute. Add the kidney beans, tomato, cayenne pepper, chilli flakes and stock and season to taste with sea salt and freshly ground black pepper. Bring to the boil, then reduce the heat to low and simmer for 30 minutes, stirring occasionally. Stir in the parsley and lemon juice and cook for a final 5 minutes. Adjust the seasoning if necessary.

• Meanwhile, prepare the cornbread. Preheat the oven to 180°C (350°F/Gas 4) and grease an 18 cm (7 inch) springform cake tin with melted butter. Sift the flour, baking powder, salt and cumin into a large bowl, then stir in the cornmeal and cheese. In another bowl, whisk together the eggs, buttermilk and melted butter. Pour the egg mixture into the dry ingredients and quickly stir until just combined; do not overmix or the bread will be heavy. Spoon the batter into the tin, smooth the surface and bake for 35–40 minutes, until the bread is golden and a skewer inserted into the middle comes out clean. Cool the cornbread in the tin on a wire rack for 10 minutes before removing.

• Put the salsa ingredients in a bowl and gently toss together. Season to taste.

• Cut the warm cornbread into wedges and place on serving plates. Spoon the bean casserole over and top with the avocado salsa. Add a dollop of sour cream if desired and serve.

SPLIT PEA SAMOSAS

preparation time 35 minutes plus 30 minutes soaking
cooking time 1 hour 20 minutes
makes 18

6 sheets frozen shortcrust pastry, thawed
1 egg, lightly beaten
plain yoghurt, to serve
mango chutney or lime pickle, to serve

FILLING
330 g (11½ oz/1½ cups) dried yellow split peas
80 ml (2½ fl oz/⅓ cup) peanut oil
2 small brown onions, thinly sliced
4 garlic cloves, thinly sliced
2 long green chillies, finely chopped
1½ tablespoons grated fresh ginger
½ teaspoon freshly ground black pepper
1 teaspoon ground turmeric
2 teaspoons cumin seeds
10 curry leaves
2 teaspoons black mustard seeds
2 teaspoons sea salt flakes
2 tablespoons lemon juice
1 large handful coriander (cilantro) leaves, coarsely chopped

- To make the filling, wash the split peas well, then place in a bowl. Cover with cold water and leave to soak for 30 minutes.

- Meanwhile, heat 60 ml (2 fl oz/¼ cup) of the peanut oil in a large saucepan over medium–high heat. Cook the onion, stirring occasionally, for 10 minutes, or until golden. Reduce the heat to medium–low and cook for 6–8 minutes, or until the onion is soft and deep golden. Add the garlic, chilli, ginger, pepper, turmeric and cumin seeds, then cook, stirring, for 2 minutes, or until aromatic.

• Drain the split peas and add them to the pan. Add 1.5 litres (52 fl oz/6 cups) water, cover and bring to a simmer. Cook for 30 minutes, stirring occasionally. Remove the lid and cook, stirring often, for a further 30 minutes, or until the mixture has a thick porridge-like consistency.

• Heat the remaining oil in a small frying pan. Add the curry leaves and mustard seeds and fry until the seeds start to pop and the leaves are crisp. Stir into the split pea mixture with the salt, lemon juice and coriander. Remove from the heat and set aside to cool to room temperature. Remove the curry leaves from the mixture.

• Preheat the oven to 200°C (400°F/Gas 6). Line a baking tray with baking paper. Cut the pastry into 18 rounds using a 13 cm (5 inch) pastry cutter. Brush the edges with beaten egg, then place 1½ tablespoons of the filling on one half of each round. Fold the pastry over the filling to form a half-moon shape, then press or crimp the edges together to seal well.

• Place the samosas on the lined tray and brush the tops with a little of the remaining beaten egg. Bake for 20–25 minutes, or until the pastry is golden and cooked through.

• Serve the samosas with yoghurt and some mango chutney or lime pickle.

SPICED SWEET POTATO COILS WITH COUSCOUS SALAD

preparation time 40 minutes
cooking time 1 hour
serves 4

2 orange sweet potatoes (about 1 kg/ 2 lb 4 oz), peeled and cut into 2 cm (¾ inch) chunks
3 garlic cloves, crushed
1 onion, chopped
2 teaspoons ground cumin
1 teaspoon ground coriander
½ teaspoon ground cinnamon
2 tablespoons olive oil
60 ml (2 fl oz/¼ cup) orange juice
100 g (3½ oz/¾ cup) walnuts, chopped
2 tablespoons coriander (cilantro) leaves, chopped
375 g (13 oz) packet filo pastry
100 g (3½ oz) butter, melted
1 tablespoon sesame seeds
1 tablespoon poppy seeds

COUSCOUS SALAD

95 g (3¼ oz/½ cup) instant couscous
2 tablespoons olive oil
1 tablespoon lemon juice
1 small handful flat-leaf (Italian) parsley, chopped
1 small handful mint, chopped
6 dried dates, finely chopped
2 teaspoons chopped preserved lemon, or to taste

- Preheat the oven to 180°C (350°F/Gas 4).

- Place the sweet potato in a bowl with the garlic, onion, spices and olive oil. Season to taste with sea salt and freshly ground black pepper and mix well to coat the sweet potato. Transfer to a baking dish and bake for 30 minutes, or until the sweet potato is cooked through. Place in a bowl and leave to cool.

- Lightly mash the cooled sweet potato using a potato masher or fork. Mix in the orange juice, walnuts and coriander and season to taste.

- Increase the oven temperature to 200°C (400°F/Gas 6). Place the filo pastry on a tray and cover with a damp tea towel (dish towel).

- Line a 35 x 27 cm (14 x 10¾ inch) baking tray with baking paper. Place one pastry sheet on a clean work surface and brush lightly with melted butter. Top with another sheet of pastry. Place one-quarter of the sweet potato mixture in a long strip 1 cm (½ inch) wide along one edge of the pastry. Gently roll up the pastry to make a cylinder, enclosing the filling. Don't roll too tightly or the pastry might split. Gently coil the cylinder into a scroll shape, then place on the baking tray and brush with butter to prevent it drying out. Repeat with the remaining pastry, filling and butter to make four coils in total. Sprinkle the coils with the sesame seeds and poppy seeds, then bake for 30 minutes, or until the pastry is crisp and golden.

- When the coils are nearly ready, place the couscous in a bowl, stir in 125 ml (4 fl oz/½ cup) warm water and 1 tablespoon of the olive oil, cover and leave to stand for 5 minutes. Fluff the grains up with a fork, then stir in the remaining olive oil and remaining salad ingredients. Season to taste.

- Serve the sweet potato coils hot, with the couscous salad.

SILVERBEET, RICE AND PARMESAN TART

preparation time 30 minutes plus 30 minutes chilling and 10 minutes standing
cooking time 50 minutes
serves 4–6

1 tablespoon olive oil
1 brown onion, finely chopped
1 garlic clove, crushed
½ teaspoon freshly ground nutmeg
250 g (9 oz) silverbeet (Swiss chard) leaves, shredded
110 g (3¾ oz/½ cup) short-grain white rice
250 ml (9 fl oz/1 cup) milk
300 ml (10½ fl oz) cream
2 egg yolks
75 g (2½ oz/¾ cup) grated parmesan cheese
50 g (1¾ oz/⅓ cup) pine nuts
rocket (arugula), avocado and cherry tomato salad, to serve

PASTRY
250 g (9 oz/1⅔ cups) plain (all-purpose) flour
2 teaspoons finely grated lemon rind
125 g (4½ oz) unsalted butter, chopped
1 egg yolk, lightly beaten with 2 teaspoons water

- To make the pastry, sift the flour into a large bowl, add the lemon rind, then rub in the butter until the mixture resembles coarse breadcrumbs. Add the egg yolk mixture and mix until a dough forms. Turn out onto a lightly floured surface and roll out the pastry to line a 22 cm (8½ inch) fluted, loose-based flan (tart) tin. Ease the pastry into the tin, then trim the edges. Cover and refrigerate for 30 minutes.

- Preheat the oven to 180°C (350°F/Gas 4). Place the flan tin on a baking tray. Line the pastry shell with baking paper, then fill with baking beads, dried beans or rice. Bake for 15 minutes, then remove the beads or rice and paper. Bake for a further 5 minutes, or until the pastry is lightly golden.

- Meanwhile, heat the oil in a large frying pan over medium heat. Add the onion and cook, stirring, for 8 minutes, or until softened. Add the garlic and nutmeg and cook for 1 minute. Add the silverbeet, then cover and cook over low heat, stirring occasionally, for 5 minutes, or until the silverbeet is tender. Transfer the mixture to a large bowl.

- In a saucepan, combine the rice, milk and 125 ml (4 fl oz/½ cup) of the cream. Stir over medium heat until the mixture comes to the boil. Reduce the heat to low, cover and cook for 10 minutes, stirring occasionally. Remove from the heat, then stir in the egg yolks, parmesan and remaining cream.

- Stir the rice mixture into the silverbeet mixture, then spoon into the pastry case. Sprinkle with the pine nuts and bake for 20 minutes, or until the filling has set. Remove from the oven and leave to stand for 10 minutes.

- Cut the tart into wedges and serve with the rocket, avocado and cherry tomato salad.

MUSHROOM, DILL AND CREAM CHEESE PASTRIES

preparation time 25 minutes
cooking time 35 minutes
serves 4

100 g (3½ oz/½ cup) long-grain rice
20 g (¾ oz) butter
1 tablespoon olive oil
500 g (1 lb 2 oz) mushrooms caps, wiped clean and finely chopped
2 garlic cloves, crushed
1 tablespoon snipped chives
250 g (9 oz/1 cup) cream cheese, softened
¼ cup finely chopped dill
1 tablespoon drained small capers
2 teaspoons lemon juice
4 sheets frozen puff pastry, partially thawed
1 egg, whisked with 1 tablespoon milk
mixed salad leaves, to serve
tomato relish, to serve

• Bring 250 ml (9 fl oz/1 cup) water to the boil in a saucepan over medium–high heat. Add the rice, stir briefly and return to the boil. Cover, reduce the heat to low and cook for 10 minutes, or until the rice is tender and all the water is absorbed. Remove from the heat and allow to stand for 10 minutes.

• Meanwhile, heat the butter and olive oil in a large non-stick frying pan and cook the mushrooms and garlic, stirring, for 4–5 minutes, until the mushrooms are tender. Remove from the heat and season with sea salt and freshly ground black pepper. Stir in the chives, then set aside to cool.

• In a bowl, beat together the cream cheese, chopped dill, capers and lemon juice. Season to taste and set aside.

• Preheat the oven to 220°C (425°F/Gas 7). Line two large baking trays with baking paper.

• Cut each pastry sheet in half. Place four pastry pieces on the baking trays. Divide the rice among the pieces, spreading it evenly and leaving a 3 cm (1 ¼ inch) border. Spoon the mushroom mixture over the rice, then dot the cream cheese mixture over the mushrooms.

• Lightly brush the pastry borders with some of the beaten egg. Place the remaining pastry pieces over each mound to cover, then press the edges together with a fork to seal. Cut three slits in each pastry top and brush with more of the egg mixture. Bake for 20–25 minutes, until the pastry is puffed, golden and cooked through.

• Remove from the oven and allow to stand for 10 minutes before slicing. Serve with mixed salad leaves and tomato relish.

GEORGIAN BEAN PIE

preparation time 25 minutes plus overnight soaking and 1 hour chilling
cooking time 2 hours 10 minutes
serves 6–8

280 g (10 oz/1⅓ cups) dried kidney beans, soaked overnight and drained
30 g (1 oz) butter
2 brown onions, finely chopped
2 teaspoons ground coriander
225 g (8 oz/1½ cups) grated mozzarella cheese
150 g (5½ oz/1 cup) crumbled feta cheese
1 large handful flat-leaf (Italian) parsley, chopped
1 large handful coriander (cilantro) leaves, chopped
mixed salad leaves, to serve

WALNUT SHORTCRUST PASTRY
300 g (10½ oz/2 cups) plain (all-purpose) flour
150 g (5½ oz/1 cup) wholemeal (whole-wheat) plain (all-purpose) flour
1 teaspoon bicarbonate of soda (baking soda)
60 g (2¼ oz/½ cup) finely chopped walnuts
200 g (7 oz) sour cream
125 g (4½ oz) butter, melted and cooled
3 egg yolks

- To make the walnut shortcrust pastry, sift the flours and bicarbonate of soda into a large bowl, returning any wholemeal flour solids to the bowl. Stir in the walnuts. In another bowl mix together the sour cream, butter and 2 egg yolks until combined, then add to the flour mixture. Using a flat-bladed knife, stir until a dough forms, adding a little iced water if the mixture is too dry. Turn out onto a floured surface and briefly knead the pastry until smooth. Form into a disc, wrap in plastic wrap and refrigerate for 1 hour.

- Meanwhile, place the kidney beans in a saucepan of water and bring to the boil. Reduce the heat and simmer for 1 hour, or until very tender, skimming off any froth. Drain well, then place in a bowl.

• Melt the butter in a frying pan over medium heat. Add the onion and cook, stirring, for 8 minutes, or until softened. Add to the beans and crush lightly using a potato masher. Stir in the ground coriander, cheeses and herbs until well combined. Season to taste with sea salt and freshly ground black pepper. Set aside to cool.

• Preheat the oven to 180°C (350°F/Gas 4). Lightly grease and flour the side of a 24 cm (9½ inch) springform cake tin, then line the base with baking paper. On a lightly floured surface, roll two-thirds of the chilled pastry out into a circle large enough to cover the base and side of the tin, then ease the pastry into the tin. Whisk the remaining egg yolk with 2 teaspoons water and lightly brush around the pastry edge. Spoon the bean filling into the pastry shell, packing it in evenly.

• Roll the remaining pastry out into a circle large enough to cover the pie, then place over the filling. Trim the pastry edges, then press to seal well. Brush the top with more egg yolk, then cut a cross in the middle of the top using a small sharp knife to allow the steam to escape.

• Bake for 1 hour, or until the pastry is cooked through and golden. Serve the pie warm or at room temperature, with mixed salad leaves.

PUMPKIN AND POLENTA CHIPS

preparation time 25 minutes
cooking time 35 minutes
serves 4

olive or vegetable oil, for brushing and deep-frying
750 ml (26 fl oz/3 cups) vegetable stock
1 teaspoon sea salt
250 g (9 oz/2 cups) coarsely grated pumpkin (winter squash)
250 g (9 oz/1⅔ cups) polenta
30 g (1 oz) unsalted butter, chopped
35 g (1¼ oz/⅓ cup) finely grated parmesan cheese
1 tablespoon finely chopped flat-leaf (Italian) parsley
1 teaspoon finely chopped rosemary

HERB MAYONNAISE

2 egg yolks
1 teaspoon dijon mustard
200 ml (7 fl oz) light olive oil
1 tablespoon lemon juice
1 handful flat-leaf (Italian) parsley, finely chopped
1 small handful basil leaves, chopped

• To make the mayonnaise, place the egg yolks and mustard in a small food processor and blend until well combined. With the motor running, very slowly drizzle in one-third of the olive oil until well combined, then add the remaining oil in a thin steady stream until all the oil has been added and the mayonnaise is a thick consistency. Add the lemon juice, parsley and basil and blend until well combined. Season with sea salt, then cover and set aside until required.

• Brush a 30 x 20 cm (12 x 8 inch) baking dish generously with oil.

• Bring the stock to the boil in a large saucepan over high heat. Stir in the salt and grated pumpkin and reduce the heat to medium–low. Gradually add the polenta in a thin steady stream, whisking constantly until smooth. Cook, stirring constantly, for 15 minutes, or until the polenta is very thick and pulls away from the side of the pan. Remove from the heat and stir in the butter, parmesan and herbs. Season to taste.

• Pour the polenta mixture into the baking dish, spreading it evenly. Leave to cool, then refrigerate for 1–2 hours, or until completely chilled and firm.

• Turn the polenta out onto a cutting board. Trim the edges and cut into 20 evenly sized 'chips', each measuring about 8 x 1.5 cm x 1.5 cm (3¼ x ⅝ inch x ⅝ inch).

• Preheat the oven to 120°C (235°F/Gas ½). Heat 1 cm (½ inch) oil in a frying pan over high heat until a small piece of polenta sizzles when dropped into the hot oil. Working in three or four batches, fry the polenta chips for 2 minutes on each side, or until golden brown, carefully turning them with a spatula. Remove and drain on crumpled paper towels. Keep warm in the oven while frying the remaining batches.

• Serve the pumpkin and polenta chips warm, with the herb mayonnaise.

OLIVE, GOAT'S CHEESE AND POTATO TRIANGLES

preparation time 30 minutes
cooking time 40 minutes
makes 16

600 g (1 lb 5 oz) desiree or other all-purpose potatoes, peeled and chopped
2 tablespoons olive oil
1 large brown onion, finely chopped
2 garlic cloves, crushed
1½ teaspoons ground cumin
35 g (1¼ oz/¼ cup) pitted green olives, chopped
200 g (7 oz) soft goat's cheese, crumbled
2 tablespoons chopped mint
2 tablespoons chopped coriander (cilantro)
2 tablespoons chopped flat-leaf (Italian) parsley
12 sheets filo pastry
60 g (2¼ oz) butter, melted

TOMATO AND MINT SALAD

250 g (9 oz) cherry tomatoes, halved
2 spring onions (scallions), finely chopped
2 tablespoons mint leaves

• Preheat the oven to 180°C (350°F/Gas 4) and line two baking trays with baking paper.

• Place the potatoes in a saucepan, cover with cold water and bring to the boil. Cook for 7–10 minutes, or until tender. Drain well, then transfer to a large bowl.

• Heat the olive oil in a frying pan over medium heat. Cook the onion, stirring, for 5–8 minutes, or until softened. Add the garlic and ground cumin and cook, stirring, for 1 minute, or until aromatic.

• Add the mixture to the potato, then mash with a fork to roughly break up the potato. Stir in the olives, cheese and herbs until well combined. Season to taste with sea salt and freshly ground black pepper.

• Place one sheet of filo pastry on a cutting board. Brush with the melted butter and top with another sheet of pastry. Repeat to make a stack of three pastry sheets. Cut the pastry stack into four 10 cm (4 inch)-wide strips. Place 2 heaped tablespoons of the potato mixture at one end of each pastry strip. Fold the bottom right corner of the pastry up to form a triangle. Fold the parcel up again along the horizontal to enclose the filling. Continue folding along the pastry strip, keeping the triangle shape. Place the triangles on the baking trays and brush the tops with a little more melted butter. Repeat with the remaining pastry, butter and potato mixture to make 16 triangles. Bake the triangles for 15–20 minutes, or until the pastry is lightly browned and crisp.

• Meanwhile, combine the tomato and mint salad ingredients in a small bowl.

• Serve the triangles hot, with the tomato and mint salad.

PIZZA WITH PEAR, RADICCHIO AND WALNUTS

preparation time 35 minutes plus proving
cooking time 25 minutes
serves 4

1 head of radicchio, trimmed, washed, patted dry and cut into quarters
60 ml (2 fl oz/¼ cup) olive oil
1 tablespoon honey
3 garlic cloves, crushed
1 teaspoon rosemary, chopped
1 large pear, halved, cored and thinly sliced
100 g (3½ oz/1 cup) walnut halves, chopped
50 g (1¾ oz/½ cup) shaved parmesan cheese
1 tablespoon ready-made balsamic glaze (see Note)
rocket (arugula) or extra radicchio leaves, to serve

PIZZA DOUGH

260 g (9¼ oz/1¾ cups) plain (all-purpose) flour, plus extra, for dusting
2 teaspoons dried yeast
1 teaspoon sea salt
1 teaspoon caster (superfine) sugar
2 tablespoons extra virgin olive oil, plus extra, for greasing

• To make the pizza dough, combine the flour, yeast, salt and sugar in a large bowl. Make a well in the centre. Combine the oil with 185 ml (6 fl oz/¾ cup) lukewarm water. Add to the flour mixture and mix until a dough forms. Turn the dough out onto a lightly floured surface and knead for 5 minutes, until smooth and elastic, adding a little extra flour if the mixture is very sticky. Place in an oiled bowl, turning to coat in the oil, then cover with plastic wrap and stand in a warm, draught-free place for 1 hour, or until doubled in size.

• Preheat the oven to 220°C (425°F/Gas 7). Lightly oil two 26 cm (10½ inch) pizza trays and dust with a little extra flour. Knock back the dough and turn out onto a lightly floured surface. Knead for 1 minute, then divide the dough in half. Roll each portion into a ball, then flatten slightly. Using a floured rolling pin, roll out each portion to a 25 cm (10 inch) round. Place the rounds on the pizza trays. Cover with a clean cloth and set aside.

• Place the radicchio on a baking tray. Drizzle with 1 tablespoon of the olive oil and season with sea salt. Bake for 5 minutes, then turn and bake for a further 5 minutes. Remove from the oven and allow to cool slightly, then remove the core and roughly chop.

• In a small bowl, combine the remaining olive oil, honey, garlic and rosemary. Brush the mixture over the pizza bases. Arrange the radicchio, pear, walnuts and parmesan over the top, then drizzle with a little more olive oil.

• Bake for 12–15 minutes, or until the bases are crisp and golden.

• To serve, drizzle with the balsamic glaze and place a few rocket or extra torn radicchio leaves in the centre of each pizza. Cut into quarters and serve.

ROCKET, BASIL AND LEEK QUICHE

preparation time 30 minutes
cooking time 1 hour 10 minutes
serves 4–6

150 g (5½ oz) rocket (arugula), stalks removed, finely sliced
185 g (6½ oz/1½ cups) plain (all-purpose) flour
125 g (4½ oz) butter, chopped
1–2 tablespoons iced water
1 tablespoon oil
1 large leek, white part only, thinly sliced
2 garlic cloves, crushed
2 eggs
125 ml (4 fl oz/½ cup) milk
125 ml (4 fl oz/½ cup) cream
basil leaves, to garnish
parmesan cheese shavings, to garnish (optional)

• Preheat the oven to 210°C (415°F/Gas 6–7). Sift the flour into a bowl. Using your fingertips, rub in the butter until the mixture resembles fine breadcrumbs. Add the water and mix to a soft dough with a flat-bladed knife. Knead on a lightly floured surface for 10 seconds, or until smooth. Refrigerate, covered in plastic wrap, for 30 minutes.

• Roll out the pastry between two sheets of plastic wrap and line a shallow 23 cm (9 inch) flan (tart) tin. Cover the pastry with a sheet of baking paper and fill with baking beads or uncooked rice. Bake for 10 minutes, remove the paper and beads and bake for 5 minutes, or until lightly golden. Reduce the heat to 180°C (350°F/Gas 4).

• Heat the oil in a frying pan, add the leek and garlic and stir over low heat for 5 minutes, or until the leek is soft. Add the rocket and stir for 1 minute. Allow to cool, then spread over the pastry shell. Combine the eggs, milk and cream and whisk until smooth. Pour into the pastry shell. Bake for 50 minutes, or until set and golden. Serve topped with basil leaves and shaved parmesan, if desired.

CORNISH PASTIES

preparation time 35 minutes
cooking time 45 minutes
makes 6

SHORTCRUST PASTRY
310 g (11 oz/2½ cups) plain (all-purpose) flour
125 g (4½ oz) chilled butter, cubed
80–100 ml (2½–3½ fl oz) iced water

165 g (5¾ oz) round steak, finely chopped
1 small potato, finely chopped
1 small onion, finely chopped
1 small carrot, finely chopped
1–2 teaspoons worcestershire sauce
2 tablespoons beef stock
1 egg, lightly beaten

• Lightly grease a baking tray. Sift the flour and a pinch of salt into a large bowl. Using your fingertips, rub in the butter until the mixture resembles fine breadcrumbs. Make a well in the centre and add almost all the iced water. Mix with a flat-bladed knife, using a cutting action, until the mixture comes together in beads. Add more water if the dough is too dry. Turn onto a floured surface and form into a ball. Cover with plastic wrap and refrigerate for 20 minutes.

• Preheat the oven to 210°C (415°F/Gas 6–7). Mix together the steak, potato, onion, carrot, worcestershire sauce and stock in a bowl and season well.

• Divide the dough into six portions. Roll out each portion to 3 mm (⅛ inch) thick. Using a 16 cm (6¼ inch) plate as a guide, cut six circles. Divide the filling among the pastry circles. Brush the edges with beaten egg and bring the pastry together to form a semi-circle. Pinch the edges into a frill and place on the tray. Brush the pastry with beaten egg and bake for 15 minutes. Reduce the oven to 180°C (350°F/Gas 4) and cook for another 25–30 minutes, or until golden.

QUICK CHICKEN AND MUSHROOM PIES

preparation time 20 minutes
cooking time 40 minutes
serves 4

50 g (1¾ oz/⅓ cup) currants
250 ml (9 fl oz/1 cup) white wine
1 sheet frozen puff pastry
2 tablespoons olive oil
2 onions, finely chopped
300 g (10½ oz) Swiss brown mushrooms, sliced
2 garlic cloves, finely chopped
1 tablespoon chopped sage
500 g (1 lb 2 oz) chopped cold roast chicken
250 g (9 oz/1 cup) sour cream
1 egg, lightly beaten
green salad, to serve

• Combine the currants and wine in a small bowl. Leave to soak for 15 minutes.

• Meanwhile, preheat the oven to 190°C (375°F/Gas 5). Invert four 300 ml (10½ fl oz) capacity ceramic baking dishs onto the frozen pastry sheet. Leaving a 1 cm (½ inch) extra border, cut around the circumference of each dish, then transfer the pastry discs to a plate, cover and refrigerate until ready to use.

• Heat the oil in a heavy-based saucepan over medium heat. Cook the onion for 5 minutes, or until softened. Stir in the mushrooms and cook for 5 minutes, or until softened. Stir in the garlic and sage, cook for 1 minute, then add the currants and wine, reduce the heat to low and cook until the liquid is reduced to 80 ml (2½ fl oz/⅓ cup). Stir in the chicken, sour cream and 1 tablespoon water and bring to a gentle boil to heat the meat through, adding a little extra water if necessary. Season with sea salt and freshly ground black pepper.

• Spoon the mixture into the baking dishes. Brush the top edge of the dishes with egg. Place pastry discs over the dishes to cover with about 1 cm (½ inch) overhanging the edges. Press to seal the pastry to the top edge of the dishes. Lightly brush the pastry with egg, then using a small sharp knife, make a few slits in the pastry to allow steam to escape. Place on a baking tray and bake for 20 minutes, or until the pastry is golden brown and puffed. Serve immediately with a green salad.

CHICKEN AND BACON GOUGERE

preparation time 40 minutes
cooking time 50 minutes
serves 6

60 g (2¼ oz) butter
1–2 garlic cloves, crushed
1 red onion, chopped
3 bacon slices, chopped
30 g (1 oz/¼ cup) plain (all-purpose) flour
375 ml (13 fl oz/1½ cups) milk
125 ml (4 fl oz/½ cup) cream
2 teaspoons wholegrain mustard
250 g (9 oz) cooked chicken, chopped
30 g (1 oz) chopped parsley

CHOUX PASTRY
60 g (2¼ oz/½ cup) plain (all-purpose) flour
60 g (2¼ oz) chilled butter, cubed
2 eggs, lightly beaten
35 g (1¼ oz/⅓ cup) freshly grated parmesan cheese

• Melt the butter in a frying pan, add the garlic, onion and bacon and cook for 5–7 minutes, stirring occasionally, or until cooked but not brown. Stir in the flour and cook for 1 minute. Gradually add the milk and stir until thickened. Simmer for 2 minutes, then add the cream and mustard. Remove from the heat and fold in the chicken and parsley. Season with pepper.

• To make the pastry, sift the flour onto a piece of baking paper. Put the butter in a large saucepan with 125 ml (4 fl oz/½ cup) water and stir over medium heat until the mixture comes to the boil. Remove from the heat, add the flour in one go and quickly beat it into the water with a wooden spoon. Return to the heat and continue beating until the mixture forms a ball and leaves the side of the pan. Transfer to a large clean bowl and cool slightly. Beat the mixture to release any more heat. Gradually add the beaten egg, about 3 teaspoons at a time. Beat well after each addition until all the egg has been added and the mixture is thick and glossy — a wooden spoon should stand up in it. If it is too runny, the egg has been added too quickly. If so, beat for several minutes more, or until thickened. Add the parmesan.

• Preheat the oven to 210°C (415°F/Gas 6–7). Grease a deep 23 cm (9 inch) ovenproof dish, pour in the filling and spoon heaped tablespoons of the choux pastry around the outside. Bake for 10 minutes, then reduce the oven to 180°C (350°F/Gas 4). Bake for 20 minutes, or until the pastry is puffed and golden. Sprinkle with a little more grated parmesan if desired.

CURRIED CHICKEN PIES

preparation time 45 minutes
cooking time 50 minutes
makes 24

PASTRY

375 g (13 oz/3 cups) plain (all-purpose) flour
1 teaspoon ground cumin
1 teaspoon ground turmeric
200 g (7 oz) butter, chopped
2 egg yolks, lightly beaten
100–115 ml (3½–3¾ fl oz) iced water
milk, to glaze

FILLING

50 g (1¾ oz) butter
1 onion, chopped
350 g (12 oz) chicken tenderloins, trimmed and finely diced
1 tablespoon curry powder
1 teaspoon cumin seeds
1 tablespoon plain (all-purpose) flour
250 ml (9 fl oz/1 cup) chicken stock
2 tablespoons mango chutney
3 tablespoons chopped coriander (cilantro)

• To make the pastry, sift the flour, cumin and turmeric into a bowl. Using your fingertips, rub in the butter until the mixture resembles fine breadcrumbs. Make a well in the centre and add the egg yolks and the iced water. Mix with a flat-bladed knife, using a cutting action, until the mixture comes together in beads. Lift onto a lightly floured work surface and gather into a ball. Wrap in plastic wrap and refrigerate for 30 minutes.

• Lightly grease two deep 12-hole patty pans or mini muffin tins. Roll out two-thirds of the pastry to 2 mm (1⁄16 inch) thick, and cut 8 cm (3¼ inch) rounds to fit the tins. Roll out the remaining pastry and cut 24 tops with a 5.5 cm (2¼ inch) cutter. Chill.

• To make the filling, heat the butter in a large saucepan and cook the onion until soft. Add the chicken and, when browned, stir in the curry powder and cumin seeds for 2 minutes. Add the flour and stir for 30 seconds. Remove from the heat and gradually stir in the stock. Return to the heat and stir until the sauce boils and thickens. Reduce the heat and simmer for 2–3 minutes, or until reduced and very thick. Stir in the mango chutney and coriander. Season and cool.

• Preheat the oven to 180°C (350°F/Gas 4). Divide the filling equally among the pastry cases and brush the edges with water. Lay the pastry tops over the pies and press around the edges with the tip of a sharp knife. Slash each top to allow steam to escape. Brush with milk and bake for 30 minutes. Cool slightly before removing from the tins. Serve warm.

CHICKEN AND LEEK PIE

preparation time 20 minutes
cooking time 40 minutes
serves 4

1 large barbecued chicken, with stuffing
30 g (1 oz) butter
1 leek, white part only, rinsed well and thinly sliced
2 carrots, finely chopped
1 garlic clove, crushed
2 teaspoons thyme
2 tablespoons plain (all-purpose) flour
125 ml (4 fl oz/½ cup) white wine
500 ml (17 fl oz/2 cups) milk, plus extra, for brushing
1 sheet frozen puff pastry, thawed
1 small handful baby rocket (arugula)
1 small fennel bulb, about 250 g (9 oz), thinly sliced
2 tablespoons olive oil
1 tablespoon white wine vinegar

- Preheat the oven to 180°C (350°F/Gas 4).

- Remove the meat from the chicken and roughly shred into a large bowl. Mix about 50 g (1¾ oz) of the chicken stuffing through the shredded chicken.

- Melt the butter in a large frying pan over medium heat. Add the leek and carrot and sauté for 5 minutes, or until softened. Add the garlic and thyme and cook, stirring, for 1 minute.

- Sprinkle the flour over and cook, stirring, for 2 minutes. Stir in the wine and bring to a simmer, stirring constantly to prevent lumps forming. Reduce the heat to low and simmer, stirring often, for 3 minutes. Add the milk and stir until the mixture simmers and thickens.

- Add the sauce to the chicken mixture and stir to combine. Spoon the mixture into a 23 cm (9 inch) round pie dish. Place the puff pastry sheet over the top, trim the edge, then crimp or pleat the edge for a neat finish. (Alternatively, use four individual ramekins or small baking dishes, and cut out four rounds from the puff pastry as lids.)

- Brush the pastry with a little extra milk. Set the pie on a baking tray and bake for 20 minutes, or until the pastry is deep golden.

- Just before serving, place the rocket and fennel in a bowl, drizzle with the combined oil and vinegar and toss gently to combine. Serve with the hot pie.

BIG BEEF AND MUSHROOM PIE

preparation time 20 minutes plus chilling
cooking time 2 hours
serves 4–6

35 g (1¼ oz/¼ cup) plain (all-purpose) flour
1 kg (2 lb 4 oz) chuck steak, trimmed and cut into 1.5 cm (⅝ inch) chunks
60 ml (2 fl oz/¼ cup) olive oil
1 large onion, finely sliced
250 g (9 oz/2¾ cups) sliced button mushrooms
2 tablespoons thyme
2 garlic cloves, crushed
275 ml (5 fl oz) beef stock
2 teaspoons worcestershire sauce
2 teaspoons wholegrain mustard
2 sheets of frozen puff pastry, thawed
1 egg, lightly beaten

• Put the flour in a shallow bowl and season well with sea salt and freshly ground black pepper. Add the steak, in batches if necessary, and toss to coat, shaking off the excess.

• Heat 2 tablespoons of the oil in a flameproof casserole dish over medium–high heat. Add the steak in batches and sear for 1–2 minutes on each side, or until golden brown, adding more oil if necessary. Remove each batch to a plate.

• Reduce the heat to medium–low. Add any remaining oil to the dish and sauté the onion for 5–6 minutes, until translucent. Add the mushrooms, thyme and garlic. Sauté for a further 2–3 minutes, or until the mushrooms have softened. Return the beef to the dish, stir in the stock, worcestershire sauce and mustard and bring to the boil. Reduce the heat, cover and simmer on medium–low for 1 hour, or until the meat is very tender.

• Transfer the beef mixture to a 1.25 litre (44 fl oz/ 5 cup) round pie dish (about 27 cm/10¾ inches across the top, 16 cm/6¼ inches across the base and 6 cm/2½ inches high). Allow to cool for 10 minutes, then cover and refrigerate for 1 hour, or until cold.

• Preheat the oven to 200°C (400°F/Gas 6). From one sheet of pastry, cut four long strips, each 5 mm (¼ inch) wide. Place the strips around the edge of the pie dish, overlapping where necessary. Brush with beaten egg, then carefully cover the filling with the remaining pastry and press the edges to seal. (Cut the remaining pastry to fill in any gaps.) Trim the overhanging pastry, brush the top generously with egg, then cut two small slits in the top of the pie to allow steam to escape. Bake for 40 minutes, or until the pastry is golden. Serve warm.

CREAMY VEAL AND ARTICHOKE PIES

preparation time 30 minutes
cooking time 1 hour 30 minutes
serves 4

1 whole garlic bulb
500 ml (17 fl oz/2 cups) chicken stock
1 leek, white part only, thinly sliced
1 celery stick, roughly chopped into 1.5 cm (5/8 inch) pieces
1 large carrot, peeled and roughly chopped into 1.5 cm (5/8 inch) pieces
2 thyme sprigs
125 g (4½ oz) small button mushrooms, halved
600 g (1 lb 5 oz) veal silverside, cut into 3 cm (1¼ inch) cubes
1 tablespoon cornflour (cornstarch)
80 ml (2½ fl oz/⅓ cup) cream
3 egg yolks
400 g (14 oz) tin artichoke hearts in brine, drained and quartered
1 teaspoon grated lemon rind
1 tablespoon lemon juice
1 small handful parsley, chopped
2 sheets frozen puff pastry, thawed

• Preheat the oven to 180°C (350°F/Gas 4). Place the garlic bulb on a small baking tray and bake for 20 minutes, or until soft when tested with a skewer. Set aside to cool.

• Put the stock in a large heavy-based saucepan and bring to the boil. Add the leek, celery, carrot and thyme, cover and simmer for 10 minutes. Add the mushrooms and veal. Season with sea salt and freshly ground black pepper. Bring to the boil, then reduce the heat and simmer, uncovered and stirring occasionally, for 30 minutes, or until meat is tender.

• In a small bowl, combine the cornflour with the cream, mixing until smooth, then stir in 2 egg yolks. Pour into the hot veal mixture and stir over low heat until thickened. Do not let the mixture boil. Remove the thyme and add the artichoke quarters. Cut the roasted garlic in half across the middle. Squeeze the garlic cloves out into the veal mixture. Add the lemon rind, lemon juice and parsley. Cool slightly.

• Preheat the oven to 200°C (400°F/Gas 6). Divide the veal mixture among four 375 ml (13 fl oz/1 ½ cup) capacity ramekins or gratin dishes and place on a baking tray. Cut 4 circles from the pastry sheets to fit over the ramekins. Place on top of the ramekins, pressing down with a fork to seal the edges. Combine the remaining egg yolk with 2 teaspoons of water in a small bowl and brush all over the pastry. Bake for 25 minutes, until the top of the pastry is puffed and golden. Serve immediately.

BEEF AND RED WINE PIES

preparation time 50 minutes
cooking time 2 hours 40 minutes
serves 6

60 ml (2 fl oz/¼ cup) oil
1.5 kg (3 lb 5 oz) chuck steak, cubed
2 onions, chopped
1 garlic clove, crushed
30 g (1 oz/¼ cup) plain (all-purpose) flour
310 ml (10¾ fl oz/1¼ cups) good-quality dry red wine
500 ml (17 fl oz/2 cups) beef stock
2 bay leaves
2 thyme sprigs
2 carrots, chopped
500 g (1 lb 2 oz) ready-made shortcrust (pie) pastry
500 g (1 lb 2 oz) block ready-made puff pastry, thawed
1 egg, lightly beaten

• Lightly grease six metal pie tins measuring 9 cm (3½ inches) along the base and 3 cm (1¼ inches) deep.

• Heat 2 tablespoons of the oil in a large frying pan and brown the steak in batches. Remove from the pan. Heat the remaining oil in the same pan, add the onion and garlic and stir over medium heat until golden brown. Add the flour and stir over medium heat for 2 minutes, or until well browned. Remove from the heat and gradually stir in the combined wine and stock.

• Return to the heat and stir until the mixture boils and thickens. Return the meat to the pan, add the bay leaves and thyme and simmer for 1 hour. Add the carrot and simmer for another 45 minutes, or until the meat and carrot are tender and the sauce has thickened. Season, then remove the bay leaves and thyme. Allow to cool.

• Preheat the oven to 200°C (400°F/Gas 6). Divide the shortcrust pastry into six portions and roll out each piece between two sheets of baking paper to a 25 cm (10 inch) square, 3 mm (⅛ inch) thick. Cut a circle from each shortcrust sheet big enough to line the base and side of each pie tin. Place in the tins and trim the edges. Line each pastry shell with baking paper and fill with baking beads or uncooked rice. Place on a baking tray and bake for 8 minutes. Remove the paper and beads and bake for another 8 minutes, until the pastry is lightly browned. Allow to cool.

• Divide the puff pastry into six portions and roll each piece between two sheets of baking paper to a square. Cut circles from the squares of dough, to fit the tops of the pie tins. Divide the filling among the pastry cases and brush the edges with some of the beaten egg. Cover with a puff pastry round and trim any excess pastry, pressing the edges with a fork to seal. Cut a slit in the top of each pie. Brush the pie tops with the remaining beaten egg and bake for 20–25 minutes, or until the pastry is cooked and golden brown.

Note *You can make a family-sized pie using the same ingredients, but substituting a 23 cm (9 inch) metal pie tin. Bake in a 200°C (400°F/Gas 6) oven for 30–35 minutes. Any remaining pastry can be rolled and used to decorate the pie, or frozen for later use.*

MOROCCAN LAMB PASTRIES WITH EGGPLANT JAM

preparation time 30 minutes
cooking time 2 hours
serves 6

600 g (1 lb 5 oz) lamb shoulder, trimmed and cut into 4 cm (1½ inch) cubes
2 tablespoons plain (all-purpose) flour
2 tablespoons olive oil, plus extra, for greasing and brushing
2 small onions, finely chopped
2 carrots, peeled and chopped
2 garlic cloves, crushed
1 tablespoon ginger, finely grated
2 teaspoons ground cinnamon
2 teaspoons ground cumin
1 teaspoon ground coriander
500 ml (17 fl oz/2 cups) beef stock
75 g (2¾ oz/½ cup) currants
1 large handful coriander (cilantro) leaves, chopped
60 g (2¼ oz/½ cup) icing (confectioner's) sugar, plus extra for dusting
2 tablespoons flaked almonds
7 filo pastry sheets

EGGPLANT JAM

2 tablespoons olive oil, plus extra, for brushing
900 g (2 lb) medium eggplants (aubergines), cut into 3 cm (1¼ inch) pieces
1 garlic clove, crushed
½ teaspoon ground cinnamon
1 teaspoon sweet paprika
1 teaspoon cayenne pepper
110 g (3¾ oz/½ cup) caster (superfine) sugar
finely grated rind and juice of 1 lemon
1 small handful coriander (cilantro) leaves, chopped

• To make the eggplant jam, heat the oil in a heavy-based saucepan over medium heat. Cook the eggplant, stirring regularly, for 10 minutes, or until soft. Add the garlic and spices and cook, stirring constantly, for 1 minute, then add the sugar, lemon rind and 60 ml (2 fl oz/¼ cup) water. Reduce the heat to low and cook for 15 minutes, stirring constantly, until the liquid has been absorbed. Stir in the lemon juice and coriander. Season with sea salt and freshly ground black pepper. Remove from the heat and cool.

• Lightly dust the lamb in flour, shaking off the excess. Heat the oil in a large heavy-based saucepan over medium heat. Add half of the lamb and cook for 5 minutes, turning often, or until browned all over. Remove to a plate and repeat with the remaining lamb. Add the onion and carrot to the pan and cook, stirring, for 2 minutes, or until the onion is soft, then add the garlic, ginger and spices, stirring constantly. Return all of the lamb to the pan with the beef stock and currants. Bring to the boil, then reduce the heat and simmer, covered, for 45 minutes, or until the meat is tender. Uncover and simmer for 20 minutes, or until most of the liquid has evaporated and the meat is falling apart. Cool, then stir in the coriander.

• Preheat the oven to 200°C (400°F/Gas 6). Combine the icing sugar and flaked almonds in a bowl. Grease six 150 ml (5 fl oz) capacity muffin holes with oil. Lay 1 sheet of pastry on a work surface, brush with oil, top with another pastry sheet, brush with oil and repeat with 2 more sheets. Using a sharp knife, cut the pastry into six 15 x 13 cm (6 x 5 inches) rectangles and use them to line the muffin holes. Divide half the icing sugar mixture among holes. Top with the lamb mixture. Layer the remaining pastry sheets, brushing each sheet lightly with oil. Using a sharp knife, cut pastry rounds large enough to cover the meat mixture, tucking in any excess pastry to enclose. Brush the tops with oil, then sprinkle with the remaining sugar mixture. Bake for 20 minutes, or until the pastry is crisp. Dust with icing sugar and serve with eggplant jam.

TURKISH PIZZA

preparation time 25 minutes plus proving
cooking time 45 minutes
makes 8

1 teaspoon dried yeast
½ teaspoon sugar
225 g (8 oz) plain (all-purpose) flour
80 ml (2½ fl oz/⅓ cup) olive oil
250 g (9 oz) onions, finely chopped
500 g (1 lb 2 oz) minced (ground) lamb
2 garlic cloves
1 teaspoon ground cinnamon
1½ teaspoons ground cumin
½ teaspoon cayenne pepper
60 g (2¼ oz/¼ cup) tomato paste (concentrated purée)
400 g (14 oz) tinned good-quality crushed tomatoes
50 g (1¾ oz/⅓ cup) pine nuts
3 tablespoons chopped coriander (cilantro)
Greek-style yoghurt, to serve

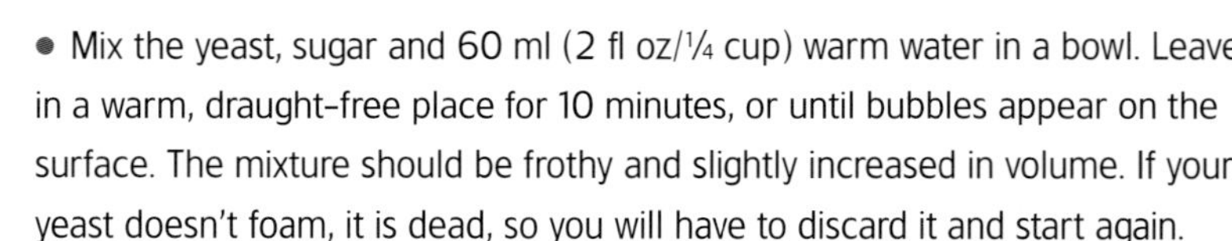

• Mix the yeast, sugar and 60 ml (2 fl oz/¼ cup) warm water in a bowl. Leave in a warm, draught-free place for 10 minutes, or until bubbles appear on the surface. The mixture should be frothy and slightly increased in volume. If your yeast doesn't foam, it is dead, so you will have to discard it and start again.

• Sift the flour and 1 teaspoon of salt into a bowl, stir in the yeast mixture, 1 tablespoon of the oil and 100 ml (3½ fl oz) warm water. Mix to form a soft dough, then turn onto a floured board and knead for 10 minutes, or until the dough is smooth. Place in an oiled bowl, cover and leave in a warm place for 1 hour, or until doubled in size.

• Heat 2 tablespoons of the oil in a frying pan over low heat and cook the onion for 5 minutes, or until soft but not golden. Add the minced lamb and cook for 10 minutes, or until brown. Add the garlic and spices, tomato paste and tomatoes. Cook for 15 minutes, until quite dry. Add half the pine nuts and 2 tablespoons of the coriander. Season, then leave to cool.

- Preheat the oven to 210°C (415°F/Gas 6–7). Grease two baking trays.

- Knock down the dough, then turn out onto a floured surface. Form into eight portions and roll each into a 12 x 18 cm (4½ x 7 inch) oval. Place on the trays. Divide the lamb mixture evenly among the bases and spread, leaving a small border. Sprinkle with the remaining pine nuts. Brush the edges with the olive oil. Roll the uncovered dough over to cover the outer edges of the filling. Pinch the sides together at each end. Brush with oil. Bake for 15 minutes, or until golden. Sprinkle with the remaining coriander and serve with the yoghurt.

GIANT SAUSAGE ROLLS WITH HOMEMADE APPLE SAUCE

preparation time 25 minutes
cooking time 1 hour
serves 4–6

1 teaspoon olive oil
1 onion, finely chopped
2 garlic cloves, finely chopped
1 carrot, finely grated
1 granny smith apple, peeled and grated
300 g (10½ oz) minced (ground) beef
300 g (10½ oz) minced (ground) pork
125 g (4½ oz/1½ cups) fresh breadcrumbs
60 ml (2 fl oz/¼ cup) tomato sauce (ketchup)
1 teaspoon mustard powder
1 teaspoon chopped sage
2 tablespoons chopped flat-leaf (Italian) parsley
2 eggs, lightly beaten
80 g (2¾ oz/½ cup) frozen peas, thawed
2 sheets of frozen puff pastry, thawed
2 teaspoons sesame seeds

APPLE SAUCE

425 g (15 oz) tin pie apples, chopped
125 ml (4 fl oz/½ cup) chicken stock
2 tablespoons vegetable pickle or fruit chutney

• Preheat the oven to 220°C (425°F/Gas 7). Line a baking tray with baking paper. Heat the olive oil in a small frying pan over medium–low heat. Add the onion and garlic and sauté for 3–4 minutes, or until softened. Add the carrot and apple and sauté for another 3–4 minutes, or until soft. Remove from the heat and leave to cool.

• Put the onion mixture in a food processor with the beef, pork, breadcrumbs, tomato sauce, mustard, sage and parsley. Process for 1 minute, or until well combined. Add half the egg and process until well mixed. Transfer to a bowl, stir in the peas and season with sea salt and freshly ground black pepper.

• Lay the pastry sheets on a lightly floured surface. Divide the meat mixture in half, then shape each half into a 'sausage' about 24 cm (9½ inches) long and 7 cm (2¾ inches) wide. Place each sausage in the middle of a pastry sheet, then roll up to enclose the filling and form two large sausage rolls. Place on the prepared tray, seam side down. Using a small sharp knife, make four incisions on top of each roll to allow steam to escape during cooking. Brush the top and sides with the remaining beaten egg and sprinkle with the sesame seeds.

• Bake for 10 minutes, then reduce the oven temperature to 200°C (400°F/ Gas 6) and bake for another 35–40 minutes, or until the pastry is crisp and golden and the filling is cooked through.

• When the rolls are nearly ready, make the apple sauce. Put the apple, stock and pickle in a saucepan over medium heat and cook, stirring, for 5 minutes, or until the liquid has reduced. Serve the sausage rolls thickly sliced, with some of the apple sauce.

CALZONE

preparation time 20 minutes plus proving
cooking time 15 minutes
serves 4

2 teaspoons dried yeast
a pinch of sugar
500 g (1 lb 2 oz/3⅓ cups) plain (all-purpose) flour, plus extra, for dusting
1 teaspoon salt
2 tablespoons olive oil
12 thin slices of prosciutto or salami
2 small handfuls of rocket (arugula)
4 marinated artichoke hearts, drained and cut into quarters
160 g (5½ oz/1⅓ cups) grated fontina cheese
200 g (7 oz/1⅓ cups) grated mozzarella cheese

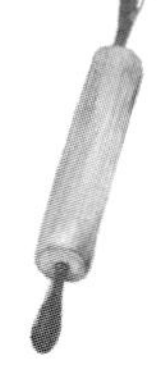

• Put the yeast and sugar in a small bowl with 150 ml (5 fl oz) warm water. Leave in a warm place for 10 minutes, or until foamy. Transfer to a large bowl, add the flour, salt, olive oil and another 150 ml (5 fl oz) warm water, then mix until a rough dough forms. Turn out onto a lightly floured surface and knead for 5 minutes, or until smooth and elastic. Place in an oiled bowl, then cover with plastic wrap and leave in a warm place for 1 hour, or until doubled in size.

• Meanwhile, preheat the oven to 200°C (400°F/Gas 6). Lightly dust a baking tray with a little flour.

• Punch the dough down, then divide into four even portions. Roll each portion out on a lightly floured surface into a 25 cm (10 inch) round about 4–5 mm (¼ inch) thick.

• Arrange the prosciutto slices over the lower half of the dough rounds, leaving a 1 cm (½ inch) border. Top with some of the rocket, then the artichoke, fontina and mozzarella.

• Brush the calzone edges with a little water, then fold the dough back over to enclose the filling. Crimp the edges together to seal well. Place on the baking tray and bake for 12–15 minutes, or until golden brown and crisp.

BAKED RICOTTA WITH PANCETTA, TOMATO AND OLIVE SALAD

preparation time 15 minutes
cooking time 40 minutes
serves 6–8

2 tablespoons olive oil, plus extra for greasing
2 tablespoons dried breadcrumbs
1 kg (2 lb 4 oz/4 cups) fresh, firm ricotta cheese
100 g (3½ oz/1 cup) parmesan cheese, grated
1 teaspoon grated lemon rind
½ teaspoon chilli flakes
1 egg yolk, lightly beaten
175 g (6 oz) thinly sliced pancetta (about 16 slices)
200 g (7 oz) mini roma (plum) tomatoes, halved lengthways
150 g (5½ oz/1 cup) pitted mixed olives
1 large handful wild rocket (arugula)
1 tablespoon balsamic vinegar (optional)

• Preheat the oven to 180°C (350°F/Gas 4). Lightly grease a 1 litre (35 fl oz/4 cup) capacity round ceramic dish with olive oil and dust with breadcrumbs, shaking out any excess. Combine the ricotta, parmesan, lemon rind, chilli and egg yolk in a large bowl. Season to taste with sea salt and freshly ground black pepper and stir to mix well. Spoon the ricotta mixture into the prepared dish and bake for 35–40 minutes or until golden and puffed. Cool slightly.

• Meanwhile, place the pancetta on a baking tray and cook in the oven for 20 minutes, or until crisp.

• Put the tomatoes, olives, rocket, olive oil and balsamic vinegar, if using, in a bowl and toss to combine. When the baked ricotta has cooled slightly, invert the dish onto a platter and cut into six or eight wedges. Serve with the tomato and olive salad and crisp pancetta.

HAM AND PINEAPPLE PIZZA WHEELS

preparation time 25 minutes
cooking time 20 minutes
makes 16

250 g (9 oz/2 cups) self-raising flour
40 g (1½ oz) butter, chopped
125 ml (4 fl oz/½ cup) milk
90 g (3¼ oz/⅓ cup tomato paste (concentrated purée)
2 small onions, finely chopped
4 pineapple slices, finely chopped
200 g (7 oz) sliced ham, shredded
80 g (2¾ oz) cheddar cheese, grated
2 tablespoons finely chopped flat-leaf (Italian) parsley

• Preheat the oven to 180°C (350°F/Gas 4). Brush two baking trays with oil.

• Sift the flour into a bowl. Using your fingertips, rub in the butter until the mixture resembles fine breadcrumbs. Make a well in the centre and add almost all the milk. Mix with a flat-bladed knife, using a cutting action, until the mixture comes together in beads. Gather into a ball and turn out onto a lightly floured work surface.

• Divide the dough in half. Roll out each half on baking paper to a 20 x 30 cm (8 x 12 inch) rectangle, about 5 mm (¼ inch) thick. Spread the tomato paste over each rectangle, leaving a 1 cm (½ inch) border.

• Mix the onion, pineapple, ham, cheddar and parsley. Spread evenly over the tomato paste, leaving a 2 cm (¾ inch) border. Using the paper as a guide, roll up the dough from the long side.

• Cut each roll into eight even slices. Place the slices on the trays and bake for 20 minutes, or until golden. Serve warm.

QUICHE LORRAINE

preparation time 30 minutes
cooking time 45 minutes
serves 6

PASTRY
215 g (7¾ oz/1¾ cups) plain (all-purpose) flour
100 g (3½ oz) chilled butter, chopped
2 tablespoons iced water

30 g (1 oz) butter
1 onion, finely chopped
3 bacon slices, finely chopped
3 eggs
185 ml (6 fl oz/¾ cup) cream
80 g (2¾ oz) grated gruyère cheese
¼ teaspoon freshly grated nutmeg

• To make the pastry, sift the flour into a bowl and add the chilled butter. Rub the butter into the flour with your fingertips until it resembles fine breadcrumbs. Make a well in the centre and add the iced water. Mix with a flat-bladed knife, using a cutting action, until the mixture comes together in beads. Add a little more water if the dough is too dry. Turn out onto a lightly floured surface and gather into a ball. Cover with plastic wrap and refrigerate for 20 minutes.

- Preheat the oven to 190°C (375°F/Gas 5). Roll out the pastry between two sheets of baking paper to fit a shallow loose-based 25 cm (10 inch) tart tin. Lift the pastry into the tin and press it well into the sides. Trim off any excess by rolling a rolling pin across the top of the tin. Refrigerate the pastry for 20 minutes.

- Cover the pastry shell with baking paper, fill with baking beads or uncooked rice and bake for 15 minutes, or until the pastry is dried out and golden. Cool slightly before filling. Reduce the oven temperature to 180°C (350°F/Gas 4).

- Melt the butter in a frying pan and cook the onion and bacon over medium heat for 10 minutes. Cool, then spread over the cooled pastry.

- Whisk together the eggs, cream and half of the gruyère cheese and season. Pour over the onion and sprinkle with the remaining gruyère and the nutmeg. Bake for 30 minutes, or until just firm.

PORK AND CHORIZO PIE

preparation time 40 minutes
cooking time 2 hours
serves 4

750 g (1 lb 10 oz) pork neck, trimmed and cut into 3 cm (1¼ inch) chunks
plain (all-purpose) flour, for dusting
2 tablespoons olive oil
2 mild chorizo sausages, cut into 1 cm (½ inch) chunks
1 large onion, chopped
2 garlic cloves, crushed
1 teaspoon ground coriander
1 teaspoon ground cumin
¼ teaspoon ground cinnamon
400 g (14 oz) tin chopped tomatoes
185 ml (6 fl oz/¾ cup) beef stock
400 g (14 oz) tin chickpeas, rinsed and drained
1 small handful coriander (cilantro) leaves

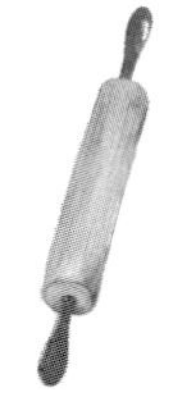

PASTRY

110 g (3¾ oz/¾ cup) self-raising flour
35 g (1¼ oz/¼ cup) polenta, plus extra, for sprinkling
a pinch of chilli flakes
50 g (1¾ oz) butter, chilled and chopped
1 egg, lightly beaten
milk, for glazing

- Preheat the oven to 180°C (350°F/Gas 4).

- Dust the pork in the flour, shaking off any excess. Heat half the olive oil in a 4 litre (140 fl oz/16 cup) flameproof casserole dish over medium–high heat. Cook the pork and chorizo in batches for 5–6 minutes, or until lightly browned all over, turning often. Remove each batch to a bowl using a slotted spoon.

- Heat the remaining oil in the casserole dish. Reduce the heat to medium and sauté the onion and garlic for 2–3 minutes, or until starting to brown. Add the ground spices and stir until fragrant. Stir in the tomatoes, stock and chickpeas, then add the pork, chorizo and any pan juices and mix well. Bring to the boil over high heat, then cover, transfer to the oven and bake for 45 minutes.

• Remove the lid and bake for a further 20 minutes, or until the pork is tender and the sauce has thickened. Remove from the oven, stir in the coriander and season with sea salt and freshly ground black pepper. Allow to cool slightly while making the pastry.

• For the pastry, put the flour, polenta and chilli flakes in a large bowl with a pinch of salt. Rub in the butter using your fingertips until the mixture resembles fine breadcrumbs. Make a well in the centre, add the beaten egg and stir using a flat-bladed knife until the mixture comes together. Turn onto a lightly floured surface and knead lightly until just smooth. Roll the pastry out so it is slightly larger than the casserole dish, then carefully place it over the top of the dish. Brush lightly with milk and sprinkle with a little extra polenta.

• Bake the pie for 30–35 minutes, or until the pastry is golden and the pork is heated through.

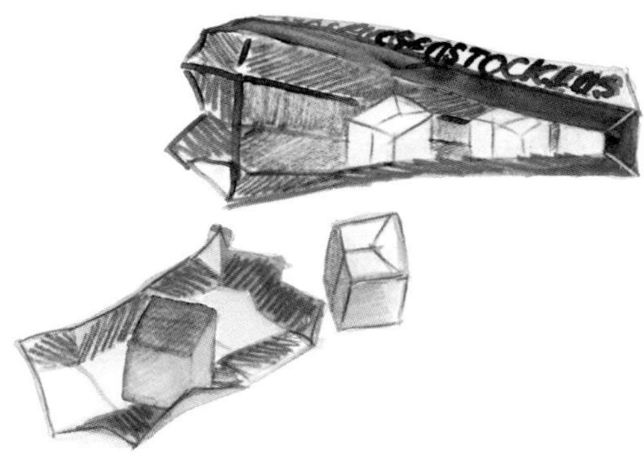

RICOTTA, PROVOLONE AND SALAMI PIE

preparation time 20 minutes
cooking time 50 minutes
serves 6

2 sheets frozen shortcrust pastry (each 25 cm/10 inches square), thawed
2 egg yolks, beaten with 1 tablespoon cold water, for glazing
250 g (9 oz) packet frozen spinach, thawed
500 g (1 lb 2 oz/2 cups) firm fresh ricotta cheese
2 eggs, lightly beaten
155 g (5½ oz/1 cup) chopped smoked cooked ham
100 g (3½ oz) chopped mild Italian salami
100 g (3½ oz) thinly sliced pancetta, chopped
110 g (3¾ oz/¾ cup) chopped provolone cheese
50 g (1¾ oz/½ cup) grated parmesan cheese
1 small handful flat-leaf (Italian) parsley, finely chopped

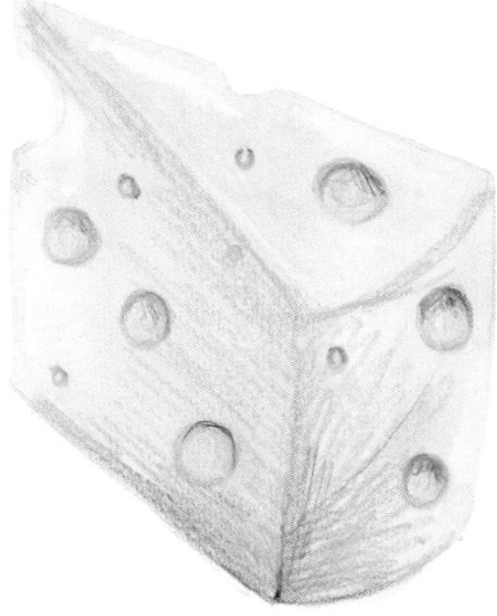

• Preheat the oven to 200°C (400°F/Gas 6). Grease a pie dish that is 4 cm (1½ inches) deep, with a 23 cm (9 inch) base and 25 cm (10 inch) top.

• Place one sheet of pastry in the pie dish, easing it in to cover the base and side. Trim the edges, using the scraps to patch up any gaps if necessary. Place a sheet of baking paper over the pastry, then fill with baking beads or dried beans. Bake for 12 minutes.

• Reduce the oven temperature to 180°C (350°F/Gas 4). Remove the beans and baking paper, then brush the pastry all over with some of the egg yolk mixture. Bake for another 8 minutes, or until the pastry is dry to the touch. Remove from the oven.

• Meanwhile, place the spinach in a colander and press firmly to extract as much liquid as possible. Place the spinach in a clean tea towel (dish towel), then wring out all the remaining liquid; the spinach should be quite dry. Place in a bowl with the remaining ingredients. Mix together well, then season with freshly ground black pepper.

• Brush a little of the remaining yolk mixture over the edge of the baked pastry base. Spread the filling over the pastry base, smoothing the surface. Cover the filling with the remaining sheet of pastry, trimming the edges and pressing them to seal, and patching up any gaps with any pastry trimmings if necessary. Brush the top with the remaining egg yolk mixture, then make a few slits using a small sharp knife, to allow steam to escape. Bake for 30 minutes, or until the pastry is golden. Serve hot or cold.

HAM BAKED BEANS WITH CHEESY CORNBREAD CRUST

preparation time 30 minutes plus overnight soaking
cooking time 2 hours
serves 4–6

300 g (10½ oz/1½ cups) dried red kidney beans
1 smoked ham hock (about 600 g/1 lb 5 oz), skin removed
1 tablespoon olive oil
1 onion, finely chopped
2 garlic cloves, finely chopped
1 green chilli, seeded and chopped
425 g (15 oz) tinned tomato passata (puréed tomatoes)
1 tablespoon treacle, golden syrup or light or dark corn syrup
2 tablespoons worcestershire sauce
2 tablespoons barbecue sauce
1 tablespoon dijon mustard
½ teaspoon freshly ground black pepper

CORNBREAD CRUST

150 g (5½ oz/1 cup) plain (all-purpose) flour
3½ teaspoons baking powder
150 g (5½ oz/1 cup) polenta
½ teaspoon sea salt
1 tablespoon soft brown sugar
250 ml (9 fl oz/1 cup) milk
60 ml (2 fl oz/¼ cup) olive oil
1 egg, lightly beaten
125 g (4½ oz/1 cup) grated cheddar cheese
125 g (4½ oz) tin corn kernels, drained well

- Place the beans in a large bowl, pour in enough cold water to cover well, then leave to soak overnight.

- Drain the beans well and place in a large flameproof casserole dish with the ham hock. Pour in enough cold water to cover, then bring to the boil over medium heat. Reduce the heat to low and simmer for 50–60 minutes, or until the beans are tender. Remove the ham hock and set aside. Drain the beans, reserving 375 ml (13 fl oz/ 1½ cups) of the cooking liquid, and set aside.

- Remove the meat from the ham hock, discard the bones and excess fat, then shred the meat using a fork. Set aside.

- Wipe the casserole dish dry, then place over medium heat with the olive oil. Add the onion, garlic and chilli and sauté for 2 minutes, then add the reserved cooking liquid, passata, treacle, worcestershire sauce, barbecue sauce, mustard, pepper, the beans and the meat from the ham hock. Simmer over low heat for 30 minutes, or until the beans are soft and tender and the liquid has thickened.

- Preheat the oven to 200°C (400°F/Gas 6).

- To make the cornbread crust, sift the flour and baking powder into a large bowl. Stir in the polenta, sea salt and sugar, then make a well in the centre. Add the milk, olive oil, egg, cheese and corn and mix together to make a dough.

- Spoon the dough evenly over the beans. Bake for 20–25 minutes, or until the crust is cooked through and golden brown. Serve hot.

PIZZA RUSTICA

preparation time 35 minutes
cooking time 50 minutes
serves 6

PASTRY
375 g (13 oz/3 cups) plain (all-purpose) flour
1 teaspoon icing (confectioners') sugar
150 g (5½ oz) chilled butter, chopped
1 egg
1 egg yolk
2 tablespoons iced water

FILLING
500 g (1 lb 2 oz/2 cups) ricotta cheese
6 eggs, separated
100 g (3½ oz) lean bacon, cut into small strips
80 g (2¾ oz) thickly sliced salami, cut into 5 mm (¼ inch) cubes
100 g (3½ oz) mozzarella cheese, grated
100 g (3½ oz) smoked mozzarella cheese or other naturally smoked cheese, cut into 1 cm (½ inch) cubes
25 g (1 oz/¼ cup) freshly grated parmesan cheese
1 tablespoon chopped flat-leaf (Italian) parsley
½ teaspoon chopped oregano
pinch freshly grated nutmeg
1 egg, beaten with 1 tablespoon cold water, to glaze

• To make the pastry, sift the flour, icing sugar and 1 teaspoon salt into a bowl. Using your fingertips, rub in the butter until the mixture resembles fine breadcrumbs. Add the egg and egg yolk and then the iced water, ½ teaspoon at a time. Mix with a flat-bladed knife, using a cutting action, to form a dough. Turn out onto a lightly floured surface and gather together into a smooth ball. Cover with plastic wrap and refrigerate for 30 minutes.

• Preheat the oven to 190°C (375°F/Gas 5) and place a baking tray on the centre shelf. Grease a pie dish with a 23 cm (9 inch) base, 25 cm (10 inch) top and 4 cm (1½ inches) deep.

• To make the filling, put the ricotta in a large bowl and beat until smooth. Gradually add the egg yolks, beating well after each addition. Add the bacon, salami, mozzarella, parmesan, parsley, oregano and nutmeg. Season well. Beat the egg whites in a large bowl until stiff, then fold through the ricotta mixture.

• Divide the pastry into two portions, one slightly larger than the other. Roll out the larger portion on a lightly floured surface until large enough to fit the base and side of the dish. Line the dish with the pastry. Roll out the second pastry portion to the same thickness for the pie lid. Spread the filling over the base and smooth the surface. Brush the pastry edges with the egg glaze and position the lid on top. Press the edges together firmly, then trim with a sharp knife. Press a fluted pattern around the rim with your fingers to further seal in the filling. Brush the surface well with the egg glaze, then prick the surface all over with a fork.

• Place the pie dish on the heated tray and bake for 45–50 minutes, until the pastry is golden and the filling is set. Loosely cover the top with foil if it browns too quickly. Set aside for 20 minutes before serving.

TUNA EMPANADAS

preparation time 20 minutes
cooking time 45 minutes
serves 2

flour, for dusting
2 tablespoons olive oil
1 small onion, finely chopped
1 garlic clove, finely chopped
½ small red capsicum (pepper), seeded and cut into 1.5 cm (⅝ inch) pieces
1 teaspoon cumin seeds
½ teaspoon smoked paprika
1 teaspoon dried oregano
1 roma (plum) tomato, seeded and cut into 1.5 cm (⅝ inch) pieces
2 tablespoons pitted green olives, chopped
2 tablespoons raisins, chopped
185 g (6½ oz) tin tuna in oil, drained
2 tablespoons chopped parsley
2 sheets frozen shortcrust pastry, thawed
1 egg, lightly beaten

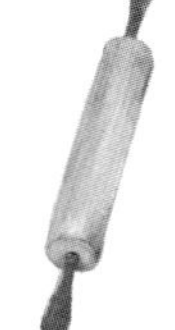

• Preheat the oven to 200°C (400°F/Gas 6). Lightly dust a baking tray with flour. Heat the oil in a frying pan over medium heat and cook the onion for 5 minutes, or until softened. Add the chopped garlic and capsicum and cook for 5 minutes. Stir in the cumin, paprika, oregano, tomato, olives and raisins. Cook for another 5 minutes, or until softened slightly. Remove from the heat, then cool to room temperature.

• Flake the tuna with a fork in a bowl, then add the tomato mixture and parsley and season to taste with sea salt. Stir to combine well.

• Cut four 14 cm (5½ inch) circles from the pastry. Spoon the filling onto one side of each circle. Dampen the pastry edges with water. Fold the pastry over the filling, to form a pastie shape. Seal the edges with a fork. Brush with the egg and make a slit on the top using the tip of a knife. Transfer the empanadas to the floured baking tray and bake for 25–30 minutes, or until the pastry is golden brown.

TUNISIAN BRIK

preparation time 30 minutes
cooking time 20 minutes
serves 2

30 g (1 oz) butter
1 small onion, finely chopped
200 g (7 oz) tinned tuna in oil, drained
1 tablespoon tiny capers, rinsed and chopped
2 tablespoons finely chopped flat-leaf (Italian) parsley
2 tablespoons grated parmesan cheese
6 sheets filo pastry
30 g (1 oz) butter, extra, melted
2 small eggs

• Preheat the oven to 200°C (400°F/Gas 6). Melt the butter in a small frying pan and cook the onion over low heat for 5 minutes, or until soft but not brown. Combine the onion, tuna, capers, parsley and parmesan in a bowl and season.

• Cut the filo pastry sheets in half widthways. Layer four of the half sheets together, brushing each with melted butter. Keep the remaining pastry covered with a damp tea towel (dish towel). Spoon half the tuna mixture onto one end of the buttered pastry, leaving a border. Make a well in the centre of the mixture and break an egg into the well, being careful to leave it whole.

• Layer two more sheets of filo together, brushing with the melted butter, and place on top of the tuna and egg. Fold in the pastry sides, then roll into a firm parcel, keeping the egg whole. Place on a lightly greased baking tray and brush with melted butter. Repeat with the remaining pastry, filling and egg. Bake for 15 minutes, or until the pastry is golden brown. Serve the pastries warm or at room temperature.

FISH WELLINGTON

preparation time 30 minutes
cooking time 1 hour 15 minutes
serves 6

40 g (1½ oz) butter
3 onions, thinly sliced
2 x 300 g (10½ oz) skinless firm white fish fillets (each 30 cm/12 inches long)
½ teaspoon sweet paprika
2 red capsicums (peppers), quartered, seeded and membrane removed
1 large eggplant (aubergine) (320 g/11¼ oz), cut into 1 cm (½ inch) thick slices
375 g (13 oz) block puff pastry, thawed
35 g (1¼ oz/⅓ cup) dry breadcrumbs
1 egg, lightly beaten
250 g (9 oz/1 cup) plain yoghurt
1–2 tablespoons chopped dill

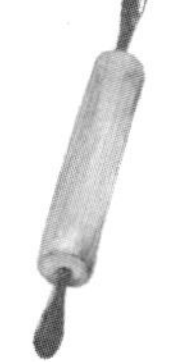

• Melt the butter in a saucepan, add the sliced onion and stir to coat. Cover and cook over low heat, stirring occasionally, for 15 minutes. Uncover and cook, stirring, for 15 minutes, or until the onion is very soft and lightly browned. Cool, then season to taste.

• Rub one side of each fish fillet with paprika. Place one on top of the other, with the paprika on the outside. If the fish fillets have a thin and a thick end, sandwich together with the thin ends on top of the thick ends so the thickness is even along the length.

• Cook the capsicum quarters, skin side up, under a hot grill (broiler) until the skin blackens and blisters. Cool in a plastic bag, then peel. Place the eggplant on a greased baking tray and brush with oil. Sprinkle with salt and pepper. Grill until golden, then turn to brown the other side.

• Preheat the oven to 220°C (425°F/Gas 7). Roll the pastry out on a lightly floured surface until large enough to enclose the fish, about 25 x 35 cm (10 x 14 inches). The pastry size and shape will be determined by the fish. Sprinkle the breadcrumbs lengthways along the centre of the pastry and place the fish over the breadcrumbs. Top with the onion, then a layer of capsicum, followed by a layer of eggplant.

• Brush the pastry edges with beaten egg. Fold the pastry over, pinching firmly together to seal. Use any trimmings to decorate. Brush with egg, then bake for 30 minutes. Cover loosely with foil if the pastry is overbrowning. Slice to serve.

• Mix the yoghurt and dill with a little salt and pepper in a bowl, and serve with the Wellington.

SEAFOOD PARCELS

preparation time 25 minutes
cooking time 35 minutes
makes 20

250 g (9 oz) skinless firm white fish fillets
100 g (3½ oz) scallops
400 g (14 oz) cooked prawns (shrimp)
30 g (1 oz) butter
1 tablespoon lemon juice
1 tablespoon plain (all-purpose) flour
250 ml (9 fl oz/1 cup) milk
60 g (2¼ oz) cheddar cheese, grated
1 tablespoon snipped chives
1 tablespoon chopped dill
10 sheets filo pastry
60 g (2¼ oz) butter, melted
2 teaspoons poppy seeds or sesame seeds

• Preheat the oven to 180°C (350°F/Gas 4). Line a baking tray with baking paper. Cut the fish into 1 cm (½ inch) wide strips. Wash the scallops and slice or pull off any vein, membrane or hard white muscle, leaving any roe attached. Peel the prawns and gently pull out the dark vein from the back, starting at the head end.

• Melt the butter in a heavy-based saucepan. Add the fish, scallops and lemon juice. Cook over medium heat for 1 minute, or until tender. Remove from the pan with a slotted spoon, place in a bowl and keep warm.

• Stir the flour into the butter and cook for 1 minute, or until pale and foaming. Remove from the heat and gradually stir in the milk. Return to the heat and stir constantly until the mixture boils and thickens. Reduce the heat and simmer for 2 minutes. Stir in the cheddar, chives, dill, fish, scallops and prawns. Remove from the heat and season to taste. Cover the surface with plastic wrap.

• Layer two sheets of pastry together with melted butter, then cut into four equal strips. Cover the unused pastry with a damp tea towel (dish towel). Place 2 tablespoons of seafood mixture on one short end of each pastry strip. Fold in the edges and roll up. Repeat with the remaining pastry, seafood and some of the remaining butter. Place the parcels, seam side down, on the baking tray. Brush with the remaining melted butter, sprinkle with poppy seeds and bake for 20 minutes.

Note *You can make the sauce a day ahead and refrigerate.*

Sweet

Desserts and sweet nibbles, from comforting classics to contemporary treats, are always worth making room for.

BANANA BREAD

preparation time 20 minutes
cooking time 45 minutes
makes 1 loaf

250 g (9 oz/2 cups) plain (all-purpose) flour
2 teaspoons baking powder
1 teaspoon mixed (pumpkin pie) spice
150 g (5½ oz) unsalted butter, softened
185 g (6½ oz/1 cup) soft brown sugar
2 eggs, lightly beaten
235 g (8½ oz/1 cup) mashed ripe bananas (about 2 bananas)
icing (confectioners') sugar, to dust

- Preheat the oven to 180°C (350°F/Gas 4). Grease and line the base of a 6 x 13 x 23 cm (2½ x 5 x 9 inch) loaf (bar) tin. Sift together the flour, baking powder, mixed spice and ¼ teaspoon salt into a bowl.

- Cream the butter and sugar in a large bowl using electric beaters until soft. Add the eggs gradually, beating thoroughly after each addition, and beat until smooth. Mix in the banana.

- Gradually add the sifted dry ingredients to the banana mixture and mix until smooth. Pour into the loaf tin and bake on the middle shelf for 35–45 minutes, or until the top is nicely coloured and a skewer inserted into the centre of the bread comes out clean. Cool in the tin for 10 minutes before turning out onto a wire rack. Dust with icing sugar.

COCONUT JAM SLICE

preparation time 30 minutes
cooking time 45 minutes
makes 20

125 g (4½ oz/1 cup) plain (all-purpose) flour
60 g (2¼ oz/½ cup) self-raising flour
150 g (5½ oz) unsalted butter, cubed
60 g (2¼ oz/½ cup) icing (confectioners') sugar
1 egg yolk
160 g (5¾ oz/½ cup) strawberry jam
125 g (4½ oz) caster (superfine) sugar
3 eggs
270 g (9½ oz/3 cups) desiccated coconut

• Preheat the oven to 180°C (350°F/Gas 4). Lightly grease a shallow 23 cm (9 inch) square tin and line with baking paper, leaving the paper hanging over on two opposite sides.

• Put the flours, butter and icing sugar together in a food processor bowl and process in short bursts until the mixture is fine and crumbly. Add the egg yolk and process until the mixture just comes together. (Alternatively, combine the flour and icing sugar in a bowl and rub in the butter with your fingertips until the mixture is fine and crumbly. Mix in the egg yolk and then gather together.) Press the dough into the prepared tin and refrigerate for 10 minutes. Bake for 15 minutes, or until golden brown. Allow to cool, then spread the jam evenly over the pastry.

• Beat the caster sugar and eggs together in a small bowl until creamy, then stir in the coconut. Spread the mixture over the jam, gently pressing down with the back of a spoon. Bake for 25–30 minutes, or until lightly golden. Leave to cool in the tin, then lift the slice out, using the paper as handles. Cut the slice into pieces. Store in an airtight container for up to 4 days.

HOT CROSS BUNS

preparation time 30 minutes plus proving
cooking time 25 minutes
makes 12

1 tablespoon dried yeast or 30 g (1 oz) fresh yeast
500 g (1 lb 2 oz/4 cups) white strong flour
2 tablespoons caster (superfine) sugar
1 teaspoon mixed (pumpkin pie) spice
1 teaspoon ground cinnamon
40 g (1½ oz) butter
150 g (5½ oz/1¼ cups) sultanas (golden raisins)

PASTE FOR CROSSES

30 g (1 oz/¼ cup) plain (all-purpose) flour
¼ teaspoon caster (superfine) sugar

GLAZE

1½ tablespoons caster (superfine) sugar
1 teaspoon powdered gelatine

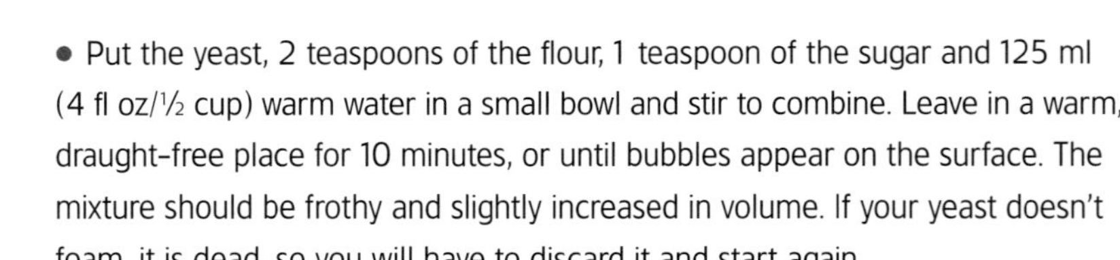

• Put the yeast, 2 teaspoons of the flour, 1 teaspoon of the sugar and 125 ml (4 fl oz/½ cup) warm water in a small bowl and stir to combine. Leave in a warm, draught-free place for 10 minutes, or until bubbles appear on the surface. The mixture should be frothy and slightly increased in volume. If your yeast doesn't foam, it is dead, so you will have to discard it and start again.

• Sift the remaining flour and spices into a large bowl and stir in the remaining sugar. Using your fingertips, rub in the butter. Stir in the sultanas. Make a well in the centre, stir in the yeast mixture and up to 185 ml (6 fl oz/¾ cup) water to make a soft dough. Turn the dough out onto a lightly floured surface and knead for 5 minutes, or until smooth, adding more flour if necessary, to prevent the dough from sticking. Place the dough in a large floured bowl, cover with plastic wrap or a damp tea towel (dish towel) and leave in a warm, draught-free place for 30–40 minutes, or until doubled in size.

• Preheat the oven to 200°C (400°F/Gas 6). Lightly grease a baking tray.

• Turn the dough out onto a lightly floured surface and knead gently to deflate. Divide into 12 portions and roll each into a ball. Place the balls on the tray, just touching each other, in a rectangle three rolls wide and four rolls long. Loosely cover with plastic wrap or a damp tea towel and leave the buns in a warm place for 20 minutes, or until nearly doubled in size.

• To make the crosses, mix the flour, sugar and 2½ tablespoons water into a paste. Spoon into a paper piping (icing) bag and pipe crosses on top of the buns. Bake for 20 minutes, or until golden brown.

• To make the glaze, put the sugar, gelatine and 1 tablespoon water in a small saucepan and stir over low heat until dissolved. Brush the glaze over the hot buns and leave to cool.

Note *These spiced, sweet, yeasted traditional Easter buns are heavily glazed and usually served warm or at room temperature. They are split open and buttered, or sometimes toasted. The dried fruit in these buns can be varied. Often, currants and chopped candied peel are used. The crosses are sometimes made with pastry instead of flour and water paste, or crosses can be scored into the dough prior to proving.*

HAZELNUT AND CHOCOLATE FRIANDS

preparation time 20 minutes
cooking time 40 minutes
makes 12

200 g (7 oz) hazelnuts
185 g (6½ oz) unsalted butter
6 egg whites
155 g (5½ oz/1¼ cups) plain (all-purpose) flour
30 g (1 oz/¼ cup) unsweetened cocoa powder
250 g (9 oz/2 cups) icing (confectioners') sugar
icing (confectioners') sugar, extra, to dust

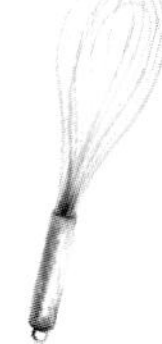

• Preheat the oven to 200°C (400°F/Gas 6). Lightly grease a 12-hole friand tin. Spread the hazelnuts out on a baking tray and bake for 8–10 minutes, or until fragrant (take care not to burn them). Wrap in a clean tea towel (dish towel) and rub vigorously to loosen the skins. Discard the skins. Cool, then process in a food processor until finely ground.

• Melt the butter in a small saucepan over medium heat and then cook for 3–4 minutes, until the butter turns deep golden. Strain to remove any residue (the colour will deepen on standing). Remove from the heat and set aside to cool to lukewarm. Place the egg whites in a clean, dry bowl and lightly whisk until frothy but not firm. Sift the flour, cocoa powder and icing sugar into a large bowl and stir in the ground hazelnuts. Make a well in the centre, add the egg whites and butter and mix to combine.

• Divide the mixture evenly among the friand holes — fill each hole to about three-quarters full. Place the tins on a baking tray and bake in the centre of the oven for 20–25 minutes, or until a skewer inserted into the centre of a friand comes out clean. Leave to cool in the tins for 5 minutes before turning out onto a wire rack to cool completely. Dust with icing sugar before serving.

HUMMINGBIRD CAKE

preparation time 30 minutes
cooking time 1 hour
serves 8–10

2 ripe bananas, mashed
130 g (4¾ oz/½ cup) drained and crushed tinned pineapple
285 g (10¼ oz/1¼ cups) caster (superfine) sugar
210 g (7½ oz/1⅔ cups) self-raising flour
2 teaspoons ground cinnamon or mixed (pumpkin pie) spice
170 ml (5½ fl oz/⅔ cup) oil
60 ml (2 fl oz/¼ cup) pineapple juice
2 eggs

ICING

60 g (2¼ oz) unsalted butter, softened
125 g (4½ oz/½ cup) cream cheese, softened
185 g (6½ oz/1½ cups) icing (confectioners') sugar
1–2 teaspoons lemon juice

• Preheat the oven to 180°C (350°F/Gas 4). Lightly grease a 20 cm (8 inch) square cake tin and line with baking paper. Place the banana, pineapple and sugar in a large bowl. Add the sifted flour and cinnamon or mixed spice. Stir together with a wooden spoon until well combined.

• Whisk together the oil, pineapple juice and eggs. Pour onto the banana mixture and stir until combined and the mixture is smooth. Spoon into the tin and smooth the surface. Bake for 1 hour, or until a skewer inserted into the centre of the cake comes out clean. Cool in the tin for 15 minutes before turning out onto a wire rack to cool completely.

• To make the icing (frosting), beat the butter and cream cheese using electric beaters until smooth. Gradually add the icing sugar alternately with the lemon juice. Beat until thick and creamy. Spread the icing thickly over the top of the cooled cake, or thinly over the top and side.

SCONES

preparation time 20 minutes
cooking time 15 minutes
serves 10–12

310 g (11 oz/2½ cups) self-raising flour
1 teaspoon baking powder
40 g (1½ oz) chilled unsalted butter, cubed
1 tablespoon sugar
250 ml (9 fl oz/1 cup) milk

• Preheat the oven to 220°C (425°F/Gas 7). Lightly grease a baking tray or line with baking paper.

• Sift the flour, baking powder and a pinch of salt into a bowl. Using your fingertips, rub in the butter briefly and lightly until the mixture resembles fine breadcrumbs. Mix in the sugar. Make a well in the centre. Pour in almost all of the milk and mix with a flat-bladed knife, using a cutting action, until the dough comes together in clumps. Rotate the bowl as you work. Use the remaining milk if the mixture seems dry. Handle the mixture with great care and a light hand. The dough should feel slightly wet and sticky. With floured hands, gently gather the dough together, lift onto a lightly floured surface and pat into a smooth ball. Do not knead or the scones will be tough.

• Pat or lightly roll the dough out to 2 cm (¾ inch) thick. Using a floured 6 cm (2½ inch) cutter, cut into rounds. Don't pat out too thinly or the scones will not be a good height. Gather the scraps together and, without over-handling, press out as before and cut out more rounds. Place close together on the baking tray and lightly brush the tops with milk.

• Bake in the top half of the oven for 12–15 minutes, or until risen and golden. If you aren't sure they are cooked, break one open. If still doughy in the centre, cook for a few more minutes. For soft scones, wrap the hot scones in a dry tea towel (dish towel). For scones with a crisp top, transfer to a wire rack to cool slightly before wrapping. Serve warm or at room temperature, with butter or jam and whipped or clotted cream.

CHOCOLATE-CHIP MUFFINS

preparation time 20 minutes
cooking time 25 minutes
makes 12

310 g (11 oz/2½ cups) self-raising flour
265 g (9½ oz/1½ cups) chocolate chips
95 g (3½ oz/½ cup) soft brown sugar
375 ml (13 fl oz/1½ cups) milk
2 eggs, lightly beaten
1 teaspoon natural vanilla extract
150 g (5½ oz) unsalted butter, melted and cooled

- Preheat the oven to 200°C (400°F/Gas 6). Lightly grease a 12-hole standard muffin tin, or line the muffin tin with paper cases.

- Sift the flour into a bowl. Add the chocolate chips and sugar to the bowl and stir through the flour. Make a well in the centre.

- Mix together the milk, egg and vanilla. Pour the liquid into the well in the flour and add the cooled butter. Fold the mixture gently with a metal spoon until just combined. Do not overmix — the batter will still be slightly lumpy. Divide the mixture evenly among the holes — fill each hole to about three-quarters full.

- Bake the muffins for 20–25 minutes, or until they are golden and a skewer inserted into the centre of a muffin comes out clean. Leave the muffins in the tin for a couple of minutes to cool. Gently loosen each muffin with a flat-bladed knife before turning out onto a wire rack. Serve warm or at room temperature.

MUESLI SLICE

preparation time 20 minutes
cooking time 50 minutes
makes 18

250 g (9 oz) unsalted butter, cubed
230 g (8½ oz/1 cup) caster (superfine) sugar
2 tablespoons honey
250 g (9 oz/2½ cups) rolled (porridge) oats
65 g (2½ oz/¾ cup) desiccated coconut
30 g (1 oz/1 cup) cornflakes, lightly crushed
45 g (1¾ oz/½ cup) flaked almonds
1 teaspoon ground mixed (pumpkin pie) spice
45 g (1¾ oz) finely chopped dried apricots
185 g (6½ oz/1 cup) dried mixed fruit

• Preheat the oven to 160°C (315°F/Gas 2–3). Lightly grease a shallow 20 x 30 cm (8 x 12 inch) tin and line with baking paper, leaving the paper hanging over on the two long sides.

• Put the butter, sugar and honey in a small saucepan and stir over low heat for 5 minutes, or until the butter has melted and the sugar has dissolved.

• Mix the remaining ingredients together in a bowl and make a well in the centre. Pour in the butter mixture and stir well, then press into the tin. Bake for 45 minutes, or until the slice is golden. Cool completely in the tin, then refrigerate for 2 hours, to firm.

• Lift the slice from the tin, using the paper as handles, before cutting into pieces. This slice will keep for up to 3 days stored in an airtight container.

ORANGE POPPY SEED MUFFINS

preparation time 15 minutes
cooking time 30 minutes
makes 12

310 g (11 oz/2½ cups) self-raising flour
40 g (1½ oz/¼ cup) poppy seeds
80 g (2¾ oz/⅓ cup) caster (superfine) sugar
125 g (4½ oz) unsalted butter
315 g (11¼ oz/1 cup) orange marmalade
250 ml (9 fl oz/1 cup) milk
2 eggs
1 tablespoon finely grated orange zest

• Preheat the oven to 200°C (400°F/Gas 6). Lightly grease a 12-hole standard muffin tin, or line the muffin tin with paper cases.

• Sift the flour into a bowl. Stir in the poppy seeds and sugar, and make a well in the centre. Put the butter and 210 g (7½ oz/⅔ cup) of the marmalade in a small saucepan and stir over low heat until the butter has melted and the ingredients are combined. Cool slightly.

• Whisk together the milk, eggs and orange zest and pour into the well. Add the butter and marmalade. Fold gently with a metal spoon until just combined. Do not overmix — the batter will still be slightly lumpy.

• Divide the mixture evenly among the holes — fill each hole about three-quarters full. Bake for 20–25 minutes, or until golden and a skewer inserted into the centre of a muffin comes out clean.

• Heat the remaining marmalade and push it through a fine sieve. Brush generously over the top of the warm muffins. Leave them to cool in the tin for a couple of minutes. Gently loosen each muffin with a flat-bladed knife before turning out onto a wire rack. Serve warm or at room temperature.

BLUEBERRY MUFFINS

preparation time 20 minutes
cooking time 25 minutes
makes 12

310 g (11 oz/2½ cups) self-raising flour
300 g (10½ oz) fresh blueberries
115 g (4 oz/½ cup) caster (superfine) sugar
375 ml (13 fl oz/1½ cups) milk
2 eggs, lightly beaten
1 teaspoon natural vanilla extract
150 g (5½ oz) unsalted butter, melted

• Preheat the oven to 200°C (400°F/Gas 6). Lightly grease a 12-hole standard muffin tin, or line the muffin tin with paper cases.

• Sift the flour into a bowl. Add the blueberries and sugar to the bowl and stir through the flour. Make a well in the centre. Mix together the milk, egg and vanilla. Pour the liquid into the well in the flour and add the butter. Fold the mixture gently with a metal spoon until just combined. Do not overmix — the batter will still be slightly lumpy.

• Divide the mixture evenly among the holes — fill each hole about three-quarters full. Bake the muffins for 20–25 minutes, or until golden and a skewer inserted into the centre of a muffin comes out clean. Leave them in the tin to cool for a couple of minutes. Gently loosen each muffin with a flat-bladed knife before turning out onto a wire rack. Serve warm or at room temperature.

Note *If fresh blueberries are unavailable, frozen ones can be used. Add while still frozen to avoid streaking the batter.*

PECAN COFFEE SLICE

preparation time 30 minutes
cooking time 30 minutes
makes 20

125 g (4½ oz/1¼ cups) pecans
175 g (6 oz) blanched almonds
2 tablespoons plain (all-purpose) flour
165 g (5¾ oz/¾ cup) sugar
7 egg whites
dark unsweetened cocoa powder, to dust

COFFEE CREAM

200 g (7 oz) unsalted butter, cubed and softened
150 g (5½ oz) dark chocolate, melted and cooled
3–4 teaspoons instant coffee powder

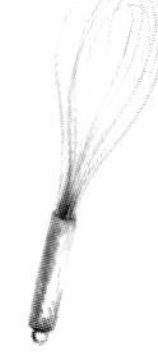

- Preheat the oven to 180°C (350°F/Gas 4). Lightly grease a shallow 23 cm (9 inch) square tin and line with baking paper, leaving the paper hanging over on two opposite sides.

- Roast the pecans and almonds on a baking tray for 5–10 minutes, or until golden. Cool slightly, then chop in a food processor until finely ground. Transfer to a bowl, add the flour and 110 g (3¾ oz/½ cup) of the sugar and mix well.

- Beat the egg whites in a large dry bowl until soft peaks form. Gradually add the remaining sugar, beating until the mixture is thick and glossy and the sugar has dissolved. Gradually fold the nut mixture into the egg mixture, a third at a time, using a metal spoon. Spoon into the tin and smooth the surface. Bake for 20 minutes, or until springy when touched. Leave in the tin for 5 minutes, then lift out, using the paper, and transfer to a wire rack to cool completely.

• To make the coffee cream, beat the butter in a small bowl using electric beaters until light and creamy. Gradually pour in the cooled melted chocolate and beat well. Mix the coffee powder with 2 teaspoons water until dissolved, then add to the chocolate and mix well. Refrigerate for 5–10 minutes for the cream to thicken slightly.

• Cut the slice in half horizontally with a sharp, serrated knife. Carefully remove the top layer and spread half the coffee cream over the base. Replace the top and spread evenly with the remaining cream. Run a palette knife backwards and forwards across the top to create a lined pattern, or use an icing (frosting) comb to create swirls. Refrigerate until firm. Trim the edges of the slice and cut into squares or fingers. Serve at room temperature or cold, dusted with dark cocoa powder or decorated with chocolate-coated or plain coffee beans, if desired. The slice can be refrigerated for up to 5 days.

PLUM AND ALMOND SLICE

preparation time 30 minutes
cooking time 1 hour 10 minutes
makes 9

- 165 g (5¾ oz) unsalted butter, cubed and softened
- 145 g (5½ oz/⅔ cup) caster (superfine) sugar
- 2 eggs
- 60 g (2¼ oz/½ cup) plain (all-purpose) flour
- 40 g (1½ oz/⅓ cup) cornflour (cornstarch)
- 2 tablespoons rice flour
- 1½ tablespoons thinly sliced glacé ginger
- 825 g (1 lb 13 oz) tinned plums in syrup, drained, seeded and halved
- 90 g (3¼ oz/1 cup) flaked almonds
- 1 tablespoon honey, warmed

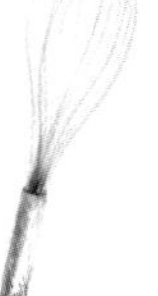

- Preheat the oven to 180°C (350°F/Gas 4). Lightly grease a 20 cm (8 inch) square tin and line with baking paper, leaving the paper hanging over the tin on all sides.

- Cream the butter and sugar in a small bowl using electric beaters until light and fluffy. Add the eggs one at a time, beating well after each addition. Sift the flours over the mixture and fold into the mixture with the glacé ginger. Spread into the tin. Arrange the plum halves on top, pressing them in. Scatter with the flaked almonds, pressing in gently, then drizzle with the honey.

- Bake for 1 hour 10 minutes, or until firm and golden. Cover with foil if the slice starts to brown too much. Cool in the tin, then lift out, using the paper as handles, before cutting into pieces. The slice can be kept for up to 4 or 5 days if stored in an airtight container in the refrigerator.

FLOURLESS CHOCOLATE CAKE

preparation time 20 minutes
cooking time 1 hour 5 minutes
serves 10–12

250 g (9 oz) dark chocolate, chopped
100 g (3½ oz) caster (superfine) sugar
100 g (3½ oz) unsalted butter, cubed
1 tablespoon coffee-flavoured liqueur
125 g (4½ oz) ground hazelnuts
5 eggs, separated
icing (confectioners') sugar, to dust

- Preheat the oven to 180°C (350°F/Gas 4). Grease a 23 cm (9 inch) spring-form cake tin and line the base with baking paper.

- Place the chocolate, sugar, butter and liqueur in a heatproof bowl. Bring a small saucepan of water to the boil, then reduce the heat to a gentle simmer. Sit the bowl over the saucepan, making sure the base of the bowl does not touch the water. Stir occasionally to ensure even melting. When fully melted, remove from the heat and mix thoroughly.

- Transfer the chocolate mixture to a large bowl. Stir in the hazelnuts, then beat in the egg yolks, one at a time, mixing well after each addition. Whisk the egg whites in a dry bowl until they form medium stiff peaks. Stir 1 tablespoon of the whisked egg whites into the chocolate, then gently fold in the rest using a large metal spoon or rubber spatula.

- Pour the mixture into the tin and bake for 50–60 minutes, or until a skewer inserted into the centre of the cake comes out clean. Leave to cool completely in the tin before turning out and dusting with icing sugar.

LUMBERJACK CAKE

preparation time 30 minutes
cooking time 1 hour 15 minutes
serves 8

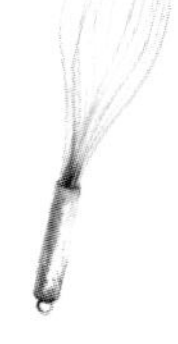

200 g (7 oz) fresh dates, pitted and chopped
1 teaspoon bicarbonate of soda (baking soda)
125 g (4½ oz) unsalted butter, softened
230 g (8½ oz/1 cup) caster (superfine) sugar
1 egg
1 teaspoon natural vanilla extract
2 granny smith apples, peeled, cored and grated
125 g (4½ oz/1 cup) plain (all-purpose) flour
60 g (2¼ oz/½ cup) self-raising flour
icing (confectioners') sugar (optional), to dust

TOPPING
75 g (2¾ oz) unsalted butter
95 g (3½ oz/½ cup) soft brown sugar
80 ml (2½ fl oz/⅓ cup) milk
60 g (2¼ oz/1 cup) shredded coconut

• Grease a 20 cm (8 inch) round springform cake tin and line the base with baking paper. Preheat the oven to 180°C (350°F/Gas 4).

• Put the dates in a small saucepan with 250 ml (9 fl oz/1 cup) water and bring to the boil. Stir in the bicarbonate of soda, then remove from the heat. Set aside until just warm.

• Cream the butter and sugar in a small bowl using electric beaters until light and fluffy. Add the egg and vanilla and beat until combined. Stir in the date mixture and apple, then fold in the sifted flours until just combined and almost smooth. Spoon into the tin and smooth the surface. Bake for 40 minutes.

• To make the topping, combine all the ingredients in a small saucepan. Stir over low heat until the butter has melted and the ingredients are well combined. Remove the cake from the oven and carefully spread the topping over the cake. Return the cake to the oven for 20–30 minutes, or until the topping is golden and a skewer inserted into the centre of the cake comes out clean.

• Remove from the oven and leave the cake in the tin to cool completely, then turn out and place on a serving plate. The cake can be dusted with icing sugar just before serving.

LEMON CAKE WITH CRUNCHY TOPPING

preparation time 25 minutes
cooking time 1 hour 20 minutes
serves 8–10

250 g (9 oz) unsalted butter, softened
200 g (7 oz) caster (superfine) sugar
2 teaspoons finely grated lemon zest
4 eggs, lightly beaten
250 g (9 oz/2 cups) self-raising flour
1 teaspoon baking powder
2 tablespoons lemon juice

CRUNCHY TOPPING
110 g (3¾ oz/½ cup) sugar
60 ml (2 fl oz/¼ cup) lemon juice

- Preheat the oven to 170°C (325°F/Gas 3). Lightly grease a 22 cm (8½ inch) square cake tin and line the base with baking paper.

- Cream the butter and sugar in a small bowl using electric beaters until the mixture is light and fluffy. Beat in the lemon zest, then gradually add the egg, beating thoroughly after each addition. Transfer the mixture to a large bowl. Using a large metal spoon, fold in the combined sifted flour, baking powder and ¼ teaspoon salt, as well as the lemon juice. Stir until the mixture is just combined and almost smooth.

- Spoon the mixture into the tin and smooth the surface. Bake for 1 hour 20 minutes, or until a skewer inserted into the centre of the cake comes out clean. Remove from the tin and turn out onto a wire rack.

- To make the topping, combine the sugar and lemon juice (do not dissolve the sugar), and quickly brush over the top of the warm cake. The juice will sink into the cake, and the sugar will form a crunchy topping. Cool.

CLASSIC SPONGE

preparation time 20 minutes
cooking time 25 minutes
serves 8

75 g (2¾ oz) plain (all-purpose) flour
150 g (5½ oz) self-raising flour
6 eggs
220 g (7¾ oz) caster (superfine) sugar
2 tablespoons boiling water
160 g (5¾ oz/½ cup) strawberry jam
250 ml (9 fl oz/1 cup) cream
icing (confectioners') sugar, to dust

- Preheat the oven to 180°C (350°F/Gas 4). Lightly grease two 22 cm (8½ inch) sandwich tins or round cake tins and line the bases with baking paper. Dust the tins with a little flour, shaking off any excess.

- Sift the flours together three times onto a sheet of baking paper. Beat the eggs in a large bowl using electric beaters for 7 minutes, or until thick and pale. Gradually add the sugar, beating thoroughly after each addition. Using a large metal spoon, quickly and gently fold in the sifted flour and boiling water.

- Spread the mixture evenly into the tins and bake for 25 minutes, or until the sponges are lightly golden and shrink slightly from the sides of the tins. Leave the sponges in their tins for 5 minutes before turning out onto a wire rack to cool. Spread jam over one of the sponges. Beat the cream in a small bowl until stiff, then spoon into a piping (icing) bag and pipe rosettes over the jam. Place the other sponge on top. Dust with icing sugar.

Note *The secret to a perfect sponge lies in the folding technique. A beating action, or using a wooden spoon, will cause loss of volume in the egg mixture and result in a flat, heavy cake.*

GINGER CAKE

preparation time 30 minutes
cooking time 1 hour 5 minutes
serves 8–10

125 g (4½ oz) unsalted butter
175 g (6 oz/½ cup) black treacle or molasses
175 g (6 oz/½ cup) golden syrup or dark corn syrup
185 g (6½ oz/1½ cups) plain (all-purpose) flour
125 g (4½ oz/1 cup) self-raising flour
1 teaspoon bicarbonate of soda (baking soda)
3 teaspoons ground ginger
1 teaspoon ground mixed (pumpkin pie) spice
¼ teaspoon ground cinnamon
165 g (5¾ oz/¾ cup) firmly packed soft brown sugar
250 ml (9 fl oz/1 cup) milk
2 eggs, lightly beaten
glacé ginger, to decorate (optional)

LEMON AND GINGER ICING
250 g (9 oz/2 cups) icing (confectioners') sugar
1 teaspoon ground ginger
30 g (1 oz) unsalted butter, melted
3 teaspoons milk
3 teaspoons lemon juice
1 teaspoon lemon zest

- Preheat the oven to 180°C (350°F/Gas 4). Lightly grease a deep 20 cm (8 inch) square cake tin and line the base with baking paper.

- Combine the butter, treacle and golden syrup in a saucepan and stir over low heat until the butter has melted. Remove from the heat.

• Sift the flours, bicarbonate of soda and spices into a large bowl, add the sugar and stir until well combined. Make a well in the centre. Add the butter mixture, then pour in the combined milk and egg. Stir with a wooden spoon until the mixture is smooth and well combined. Pour into the tin and smooth the surface. Bake for 45–60 minutes, until a skewer inserted into the centre of the cake comes out clean. Leave in the tin for 20 minutes before turning out onto a wire rack to cool.

• To make the icing (frosting), sift the icing sugar into a small heatproof bowl and stir in the ground ginger, butter, milk, lemon juice and zest until the mixture forms a smooth paste. Stand the bowl over a saucepan of simmering water, making sure the base of the bowl does not touch the water. Stir until smooth and glossy, then remove from the heat. Spread over the cake and decorate the top with glacé ginger, if desired.

Note *This delicious ginger cake can be served the day it is baked but it is best served two or three days after baking so the flavours have time to develop. It will store well for up to a week in an airtight container, or can be frozen, un-iced, for up to 3 months. It can also be served un-iced and decorated by lightly dusting the top with sifted icing sugar.*

VANILLA SLICE

preparation time 40 minutes
cooking time 15 minutes
makes 9

500 g (1 lb 2 oz) block ready-made puff pastry, thawed
230 g (8½ oz/1 cup) caster (superfine) sugar
90 g (3¼ oz/¾ cup) cornflour (cornstarch)
60 g (2¼ oz/½ cup) custard powder or instant vanilla pudding mix
1 litre (35 fl oz/4 cups) cream
60 g (2¼ oz) unsalted butter, cubed
2 teaspoons natural vanilla extract
3 egg yolks

ICING
185 g (6½ oz/1½ cups) icing (confectioners') sugar
60 g (2¼ oz) passionfruit pulp
15 g (½ oz) unsalted butter, melted

• Preheat the oven to 210°C (415°F/Gas 6–7). Grease two baking trays with oil. Line the base and sides of a shallow 23 cm (9 inch) square cake tin with foil, leaving the foil hanging over on two opposite sides. Divide the pastry in half, roll each piece to a 25 cm (10 inch) square about 3 mm (1/8 inch) thick and place on the prepared trays. Prick all over with a fork and bake for 8 minutes, or until golden. Trim each pastry sheet to a 23 cm (9 inch) square. Place one sheet, top side down, in the cake tin.

• Combine the sugar, cornflour and custard powder in a saucepan. Gradually add the cream and stir until smooth. Stir over medium heat for 2 minutes, or until the mixture boils and thickens. Add the butter and vanilla and stir until smooth. Remove from the heat and whisk in the egg yolks until the mixture is combined. Spread the custard over the cooled pastry in the tin and cover with the remaining pastry, top side down. Allow to cool.

• To make the icing (frosting), combine the icing sugar, passionfruit pulp and butter in a small bowl and stir together until smooth.

• Lift the slice out of the tin, using the foil as handles, spread the icing over the top and leave it to set before carefully cutting into squares with a serrated knife.

SWEDISH TEA RING

preparation time 1 hour plus proving
cooking time 30 minutes
serves 10–12

2 teaspoons dried yeast
170 ml (5½ fl oz/⅔ cup) milk
60 g (2¼ oz) unsalted butter, softened
2 tablespoons caster (superfine) sugar
375 g (13 oz/3 cups) plain (all-purpose) flour
1 egg, lightly beaten
1 egg yolk, extra

FILLING
30 g (1 oz) unsalted butter
1 tablespoon caster (superfine) sugar
100 g (3½ oz) roughly ground blanched almonds
95 g (3½ oz/½ cup) mixed dried fruit
105 g (3¾ oz/½ cup) glacé cherries, halved

ICING
125 g (4½ oz/1 cup) icing (confectioners') sugar
1–2 tablespoons milk
2 drops natural almond extract

• Lightly grease a baking tray or line with baking paper. Dissolve the yeast in 2 tablespoons warm water in a bowl. Leave in a warm, draught-free place for 10 minutes, or until bubbles appear on the surface. The mixture should be frothy and slightly increased in volume. If your yeast doesn't foam, it is dead, so you will have to discard it and start again. Heat the milk, butter, sugar and ½ teaspoon salt in a saucepan until just warmed.

• Sift 250 g (9 oz/2 cups) of the flour into a large bowl. Add the yeast and milk mixtures and beaten egg and mix to a smooth batter. Add enough of the remaining flour to make a soft dough. Turn out onto a lightly floured surface and knead for 10 minutes, or until the dough is smooth and elastic. Place the dough in a large, lightly oiled bowl and brush the dough with oil. Cover with plastic wrap or a damp tea towel (dish towel) and leave in a warm place for 1 hour, or until well risen.

• Meanwhile, to make the filling, cream the butter and sugar using electric beaters until light and fluffy, then mix in the almonds, mixed dried fruit and cherries.

• Punch the dough down and knead for 1 minute. Roll the dough to a 25 x 45 cm (10 x 17¾ inch) rectangle. Spread the filling over the dough, leaving a 2 cm (¾ inch) border. Roll up and form into a ring with the seam underneath. Mix the egg yolk with 1 tablespoon water and use to seal the ends together. Place on the tray. Snip with scissors from the outside edge at 4 cm (1½ inch) intervals. Cut towards the centre of the ring, about two-thirds of the way in. Turn the cut pieces on the side and flatten slightly, giving it a petal-like appearance. Cover the tea ring with plastic wrap and leave in a warm place for 45 minutes, or until well risen.

• Preheat the oven to 180°C (350°F/Gas 4). Brush the tea ring with some of the egg yolk and water and bake for 20–25 minutes, or until firm and golden. Cover with foil if the tea cake is browning too much. Remove and cool.

• To make the icing (frosting), combine the ingredients until smooth. Drizzle over the tea ring.

FINGER BUNS

preparation time 45 minutes plus proving
cooking time 15 minutes
serves 12

500 g (1 lb 2 oz/4 cups) plain (all-purpose) flour
35 g (1¼ oz/⅓ cup) milk powder
1 tablespoon dried yeast
115 g (4 oz/½ cup) caster (superfine) sugar
60 g (2¼ oz/½ cup) sultanas (golden raisins)
60 g (2¼ oz) unsalted butter, melted
1 egg, lightly beaten
1 egg yolk, extra, to glaze

GLACE ICING

155 g (5½ oz/1¼ cups) icing (confectioners') sugar
20 g (¾ oz) unsalted butter, melted
pink food colouring

- Mix 375 g (13 oz/3 cups) of the flour with the milk powder, yeast, caster sugar, sultanas and ½ teaspoon salt in a large bowl. Make a well in the centre. Combine the butter, egg and 250 ml (9 fl oz/1 cup) warm water and add all at once to the flour. Stir for 2 minutes, or until well combined. Add enough of the remaining flour to make a soft dough.

- Turn out onto a lightly floured surface. Knead for 10 minutes, or until the dough is smooth and elastic, adding more flour if necessary. Place in a large lightly oiled bowl and brush with oil. Cover with plastic wrap and leave in a warm place for 1 hour, or until well risen.

• Lightly grease two large baking trays. Preheat the oven to 180°C (350°F/Gas 4). Punch down the dough and knead for 1 minute, then divide into 12 pieces and shape each piece into a 15 cm (6 inch) long oval. Put the ovals on the trays, 5 cm (2 inches) apart. Cover with plastic wrap and set aside in a warm place for 20–25 minutes, or until well risen.

• Mix the extra egg yolk with 1 ½ teaspoons water and brush over the dough. Bake for 12–15 minutes, or until firm and golden. Transfer to a wire rack to cool.

• To make the icing (frosting), stir the icing sugar, 2–3 teaspoons water and the melted butter together in a bowl until smooth. Mix in the food colouring and spread over the tops of the buns. Finger buns are delicious buttered.

PINEAPPLE UPSIDE-DOWN CAKE

preparation time 30 minutes
cooking time 1 hour
serves 8

90 g (3¼ oz) unsalted butter, melted
95 g (3½ oz/½ cup) soft brown sugar
440 g (15½ oz) tinned pineapple rings in natural juice
6 red glacé cherries
125 g (4½ oz) unsalted butter, extra, softened
170 g (6 oz/¾ cup) caster (superfine) sugar
2 eggs, lightly beaten
1 teaspoon natural vanilla extract
185 g (6½ oz/1½ cups) self-raising flour
60 g (2¼ oz/½ cup) plain (all-purpose) flour
30 g (1 oz/⅓ cup) desiccated coconut

• Preheat the oven to 180°C (350°F/Gas 4). Pour the melted butter into a 20 cm (8 inch) round tin, brushing some of it up the side, but leaving most of it on the base. Sprinkle the brown sugar over the base. Drain the pineapple, reserving 125 ml (4 fl oz/½ cup) of the juice. Arrange the pineapple rings in the base of the tin (five on the outside and one in the centre) and place a cherry in the centre of each ring.

• Cream the extra butter and sugar in a small bowl using electric beaters until light and fluffy. Add the egg gradually, beating thoroughly after each addition. Add the vanilla and beat until combined. Transfer to a large bowl. Using a metal spoon, fold in the sifted flours, then add the coconut and reserved pineapple juice. Stir until the mixture is just combined and almost smooth. Spoon the mixture into the tin over the pineapple rings, then smooth the surface. Indent the centre slightly with the back of a spoon to ensure the cake has a reasonably flat base. Bake for 50–60 minutes, or until a skewer inserted into the centre of the cake comes out clean. Leave the cake in the tin for 10 minutes before turning out onto a wire rack to cool.

BOILED FRUIT CAKE

preparation time 30 minutes
cooking time 1 hour 30 minutes
serves 8–10

250 g (9 oz) unsalted butter
185 g (6½ oz/1 cup) soft brown sugar
1 kg (2 lb 4 oz) mixed dried fruit
125 ml (4 fl oz/½ cup) sweet sherry
½ teaspoon bicarbonate of soda (baking soda)
185 g (6½ oz/1½ cups) self-raising flour
125 g (4½ oz/1 cup) plain (all-purpose) flour
1 teaspoon ground mixed (pumpkin pie) spice
4 eggs, lightly beaten

• Preheat the oven to 180°C (350°F/Gas 4). Lightly grease and line a 22 cm (8½ inch) round cake tin.

• Put the butter, sugar, mixed fruit, sherry and 185 ml (6 fl oz/¾ cup) water in a saucepan. Stir over low heat until the butter has melted and the sugar has dissolved. Bring to the boil, reduce the heat and simmer for 10 minutes. Remove from the heat, stir in the bicarbonate of soda and cool.

• Sift the flours and spice into a large bowl and make a well in the centre. Add the egg to the fruit, mix well, then pour into the well and mix thoroughly. Pour into the tin and smooth the surface. Wrap the outside of the tin and sit the cake tin on several layers of newspaper in the oven. Bake for 1–1¼ hours, or until a skewer inserted into the centre of the cake comes out clean. Leave in the tin for at least an hour before turning out onto a wire rack. The flavour improves after standing for 3 days.

CARROT CAKE

preparation time 40 minutes
cooking time 1 hour 30 minutes
serves 8–10

125 g (4½ oz/1 cup) self-raising flour
125 g (4½ oz/1 cup) plain (all-purpose) flour
2 teaspoons ground cinnamon
1 teaspoon ground ginger
½ teaspoon freshly grated nutmeg
1 teaspoon bicarbonate of soda (baking soda)
250 ml (9 fl oz/1 cup) oil
185 g (6½ oz/1 cup) soft brown sugar
4 eggs
175 g (6 oz/½ cup) golden syrup or dark corn syrup
390 g (13¾ oz/2½ cups) grated carrot
60 g (2¼ oz/½ cup) chopped pecans
freshly grated nutmeg, extra, to sprinkle

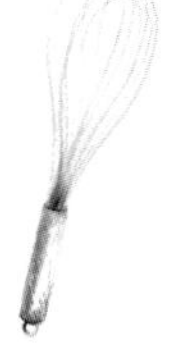

LEMON ICING

175 g (6 oz) cream cheese, softened
60 g (2¼ oz) unsalted butter, softened
185 g (6½ oz/1½ cups) icing (confectioners') sugar
1 teaspoon natural vanilla extract
1–2 teaspoons lemon juice

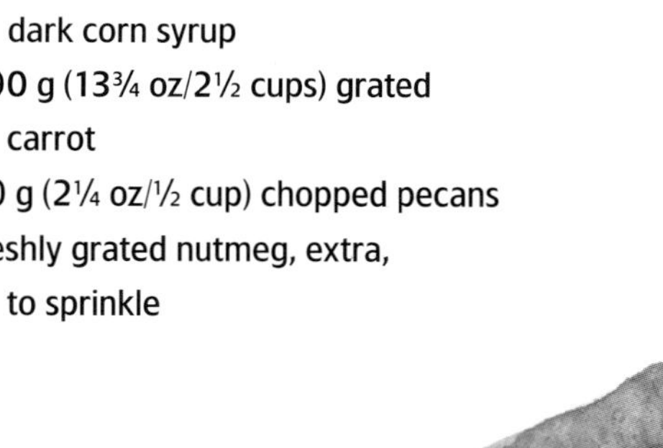

- Preheat the oven to 160°C (315°F/Gas 2–3). Lightly grease a 23 cm (9 inch) round cake tin and line the base and side with baking paper.

- Sift the flours, cinnamon, ginger, nutmeg and bicarbonate of soda into a large bowl and make a well in the centre.

- Whisk together the oil, sugar, eggs and golden syrup until combined. Add this mixture to the well in the flour and gradually stir with a metal spoon until smooth. Stir in the carrot and nuts, spoon into the tin and smooth the surface. Bake for 1½ hours, until a skewer inserted into the centre of the cake comes out clean. Leave the cake in the tin for at least 15 minutes before turning out onto a wire rack to cool completely.

- To make the icing (frosting), beat the cream cheese and butter using electric beaters until smooth. Gradually add the icing sugar alternately with the vanilla and lemon juice, beating until light and creamy. Spread the icing over the cake using a flat-bladed knife. Sprinkle with freshly grated nutmeg.

LIME AND COCONUT SHORTCAKES

preparation time 30 minutes
cooking time 30 minutes
serves 6

45 g (1½ oz/¾ cup) shredded coconut
250 g (9 oz/1⅔ cups) plain (all-purpose) flour, plus extra, for dusting
2 teaspoons baking powder
115 g (4 oz/½ cup) caster (superfine) sugar
65 g (2½ oz/¾ cup) desiccated coconut
150 g (5½ oz) unsalted butter, chopped
1 egg, lightly beaten
1 teaspoon coconut essence
210 g (7½ oz/⅔ cup) lime marmalade
softly whipped cream, to serve

- Preheat the oven to 170°C (325°F/Gas 3). Spread the shredded coconut on a baking tray and toast in the oven for 6–7 minutes, or until light golden. Cool the coconut and set aside.

- Lightly grease and flour 6 holes of a standard non-stick muffin or friand tin. Line each hole with a circle of baking paper. Sift the flour and baking powder into a bowl, then stir in the sugar and desiccated coconut. Rub in the butter until the mixture resembles coarse breadcrumbs. Make a well in the centre, add the egg and coconut essence and, using a fork, stir the egg into the flour mixture until a coarse dough forms. Turn out onto a lightly floured board and knead briefly until smooth.

• Take about 2 heaped tablespoons of the dough and, using your hands, form into a circle about 5 mm (¼ inch) thick. Use the circle to line one of the muffin holes, trimming the edge. Repeat until the 6 muffin holes are lined with dough. Place 1 tablespoon of marmalade in each hole. Divide the remaining dough, including any trimmings, into 6 even pieces and press each piece into a round large enough to cover each shortcake. Press the edges of the pastry together to seal, then bake for 20 minutes, or until golden. Cool the shortcakes in the muffin tin for 10 minutes, then carefully turn out onto a wire rack to serve or to cool completely.

• To serve, place the shortcakes on serving plates, add a generous dollop of cream and sprinkle with toasted coconut.

DATE, RAISIN AND PECAN LOAF

preparation time 30 minutes
cooking time 20 minutes
makes 1 loaf

240 g (8½ oz/1½ cups) chopped pitted dates
125 g (4½ oz/1 cup) raisins
30 g (1 oz) unsalted butter, chopped
60 g (2¼ oz/⅓ cup) soft brown sugar
300 g (10½ oz/2 cups) self-raising flour
1 teaspoon mixed (pumpkin pie) spice
1 egg, lightly beaten
1 tablespoon vegetable oil
1 tablespoon golden syrup or dark corn syrup
60 ml (2 fl oz/¼ cup) milk
100 g (3½ oz/1 cup) pecans, roughly chopped
assorted cheeses, to serve
grapes, to serve
quince or guava paste, to serve (optional)

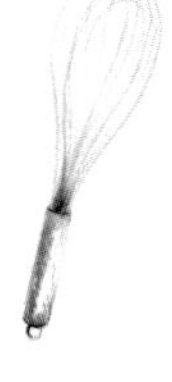

- Preheat the oven to 160°C (315°F/Gas 2–3). Lightly grease a 1.5 litre (52 fl oz/6 cup) loaf (bar) tin (measuring about 10.5 x 21 cm/4 x 8¼ inches) and line the base with baking paper.

- Put the dates, raisins, butter and sugar in a large bowl. Pour 150 ml (5 fl oz) boiling water over, stirring to melt the butter and to dissolve the sugar. Leave to stand for 5 minutes for the fruit to absorb some of the liquid.

- Sift the flour and mixed spice into a large bowl. In a small bowl, whisk the egg, oil, golden syrup and milk until well combined, then pour into the flour mixture, stirring until a smooth batter forms. Stir the fruit mixture and pecans through, then pour into the loaf tin, smoothing the surface.

- Bake for 50 minutes, or until a cake tester inserted in the centre of the loaf comes out clean. Leave to cool for 10 minutes before turning out onto a wire rack to cool completely. Wrap the loaf in plastic wrap and leave for several hours or overnight before cutting into thin slices.

- Serve with a cheese platter, grapes, and quince or guava paste if desired.

WHITE CHOCOLATE AND PASSIONFRUIT CHEESECAKE

preparation time 30 minutes plus 1 hour 30 minutes standing
cooking time 1 hour
serves 10–12

150 g (5½ oz) plain sweet digestive biscuits (cookies), broken
90 g (3¼ oz/1 cup) desiccated coconut
80 g (2¾ oz) unsalted butter, melted
250 g (9 oz) good-quality white chocolate, chopped
500 g (1 lb 2 oz) cream cheese, softened
250 g (9 oz/1 cup) sour cream
170 g (5¾ oz/¾ cup) caster (superfine) sugar
2 teaspoons natural vanilla extract
3 eggs, lightly beaten
2 x 170 ml (5½ fl oz) tins passionfruit pulp

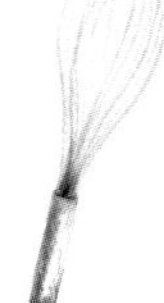

- Preheat the oven to 160°C (315°F/Gas 2–3). Line the base of a 22 cm (8½ inch) springform tin with baking paper.

- Place the biscuits in a food processor and process until they resemble breadcrumbs. Add the coconut and melted butter and process until well combined. Press the mixture over the base of the pan, then refrigerate for 30 minutes.

- Place the white chocolate in a small heatproof bowl, then place the bowl over a small saucepan of simmering water, taking care that the water does not touch the base of the bowl. Heat until the chocolate has melted, then remove from the heat and stir until smooth. Set aside until cool.

• Place the cream cheese, sour cream, sugar and vanilla in a food processor bowl. Process until smooth, add the eggs and process until just combined. Take care not to over-process the eggs. Add the chocolate and half the passionfruit and, using the pulse button, process until just combined. Pour the mixture over the biscuit base in the tin, smoothing the top.

• Place a dish of boiling water in the bottom of the oven to help prevent the cheesecake from cracking, then bake the cheesecake for 1 hour, or until just firm in the centre. Turn the oven off, open the door slightly and cool the cake in the oven for 1 hour. Remove, cool to room temperature, then chill. Serve drizzled with the extra passionfruit pulp.

NEW YORK CHEESECAKE

preparation time 1 hour
cooking time 1 hour 50 minutes
serves 10–12

60 g (2¼ oz/½ cup) self-raising flour
125 g (4½ oz/1 cup) plain (all-purpose) flour
55 g (2 oz/¼ cup) caster (superfine) sugar
1 teaspoon grated lemon zest
80 g (2¾ oz) unsalted butter, chopped
1 egg
375 ml (13 fl oz/1½ cups) cream, to serve

FILLING
750 g (1 lb 10 oz/3 cups) cream cheese, softened
230 g (8½ oz/1 cup) caster (superfine) sugar
30 g (1 oz/¼ cup) plain (all-purpose) flour
2 teaspoons grated orange zest
2 teaspoons grated lemon zest
4 eggs
170 ml (5½ fl oz/⅔ cup) cream

CANDIED ZEST
finely shredded zest of 3 limes, 3 lemons and 3 oranges
230 g (8½ oz/1 cup) caster (superfine) sugar

• Preheat the oven to 210°C (415°F/Gas 6–7). Lightly grease a 23 cm (9 inch) springform cake tin.

• To make the pastry, combine the flours, sugar, lemon zest and butter for about 30 seconds in a food processor, until crumbly. Add the egg and process briefly until the mixture just comes together. Turn out onto a lightly floured surface and gather together into a ball. Refrigerate in plastic wrap for about 20 minutes, or until the mixture is firm.

• Roll the dough between two sheets of baking paper until large enough to fit the base and side of the tin. Ease into the tin and trim the edges. Cover the pastry with baking paper, then baking beads or uncooked rice. Bake for 10 minutes, then remove the baking paper and rice. Flatten the pastry lightly with the back of a spoon and bake for another 5 minutes. Set aside to cool.

• To make the filling, reduce the oven to 150°C (300°F/Gas 2). Beat the cream cheese, sugar, flour and orange and lemon zest until smooth. Add the eggs, one at a time, beating after each addition. Beat in the cream, pour over the pastry and bake for 1½ hours, or until almost set. Turn off the oven and leave to cool with the door ajar. When cool, refrigerate.

• To make the candied zest, place a little water in a saucepan with the lime, lemon and orange zest, bring to the boil and simmer for 1 minute. Drain the zest and repeat with fresh water. This will get rid of any bitterness in the zest and syrup. Put the sugar in a saucepan with 60 ml (2 fl oz/¼ cup) water and stir over low heat until dissolved. Add the zest, bring to the boil, then reduce the heat and simmer for 5–6 minutes, or until the zest is translucent. Allow to cool, drain the zest and place on baking paper to dry (you can save the syrup to serve with the cheesecake).

• Whip the cream, spoon over the cold cheesecake and top with candied zest.

Note *To make the cheesecake easier to cut, heap the zest in mounds, then cut between the mounds of zest.*

RHUBARB LATTICE PIE

preparation time 35 minutes
cooking time 1 hour
serves 4–6

RHUBARB FILLING
500 g (1 lb 2 oz) rhubarb, trimmed, leaves discarded
115 g (4 oz/½ cup) caster (superfine) sugar
5 cm (2 inch) piece orange zest, pith removed
1 tablespoon orange juice
410 g (14½ oz) tinned pie apples
caster (superfine) sugar, extra, to taste

150 g (5½ oz/1¼ cups) plain (all-purpose) flour
¼ teaspoon baking powder
90 g (3¼ oz) chilled unsalted butter, cubed
1 tablespoon caster (superfine) sugar
80–100 ml (2½–3½ fl oz) iced water
milk, to glaze
raw (demerara) sugar, to decorate

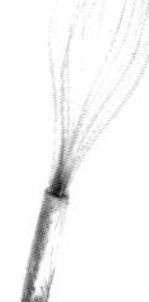

• To make the rhubarb filling, preheat the oven to 180°C (350°F/Gas 4). Cut the rhubarb into 3 cm (1¼ inch) lengths and combine in a large casserole dish with the sugar, orange zest and juice. Cover the dish with a lid or foil and bake for 30 minutes, or until the rhubarb is just tender. Drain away any excess juice and discard the zest. Cool, then stir in the apple. Add more sugar to taste.

• While the rhubarb is cooking, sift the flour and baking powder into a bowl. Using your fingertips, rub in the cubed butter until the mixture resembles fine breadcrumbs. Stir in the sugar. Make a well in the centre and add almost all the water. Mix with a flat-bladed knife, using a cutting action, until the mixture comes together in beads. Add some more water if the dough is too dry. Gather together, wrap in plastic wrap and chill for 20 minutes.

• Roll the pastry out between two sheets of baking paper to a 28 cm (11 ¼ inch) circle. Cut the pastry into 1.5 cm (5/8 inch) strips, using a sharp knife or a fluted cutter. Lay half the strips on a sheet of baking paper, leaving a 1 cm (½ inch) gap between each strip. Interweave the remaining strips to form a lattice. Cover with plastic wrap and refrigerate, flat, for 20 minutes.

• Increase the oven to 210°C (415°F/Gas 6–7). Pour the filling into a 20 cm (8 inch) pie dish and smooth the surface. Invert the pastry lattice on the pie, remove the paper and trim the pastry edge. Bake for 10 minutes. Remove from the oven, brush with milk and sprinkle with sugar. Reduce the oven to 180°C (350°F/Gas 4) and bake the pie for 20 minutes, or until the pastry is golden and the filling is bubbling.

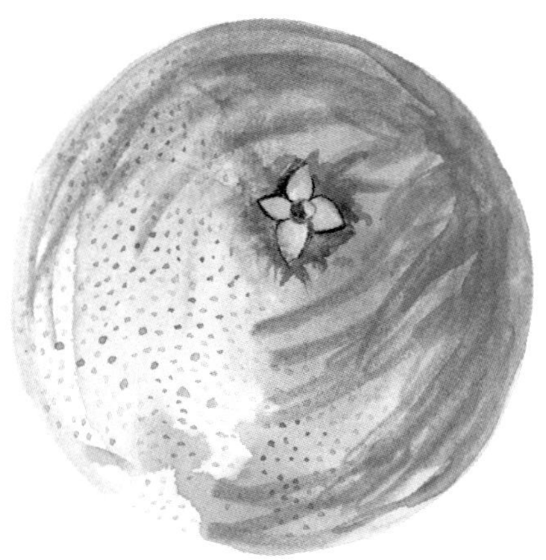

APPLE PIE

preparation time 45 minutes
cooking time 50 minutes
serves 6

FILLING

6 large granny smith apples, peeled, cored and cut into wedges
2 tablespoons caster (superfine) sugar
1 teaspoon finely grated lemon zest
pinch ground cloves

PASTRY

250 g (9 oz/2 cups) plain (all-purpose) flour
30 g (1 oz/¼ cup) self-raising flour
150 g (5½ oz) chilled unsalted butter, cubed
2 tablespoons caster (superfine) sugar
80–100 ml (2½–3½ fl oz) iced water

2 tablespoons marmalade
1 egg, lightly beaten
1 tablespoon sugar

- Lightly grease a 23 cm (9 inch) pie dish.

- To make the filling, put the apple in a saucepan with the sugar, lemon zest, cloves and 2 tablespoons water. Cover and cook over low heat for 8 minutes, or until the apple is just tender, shaking the pan occasionally. Drain the apple and cool completely.

- To make the pastry, sift the flours into a bowl. Using your fingertips, rub in the butter until the mixture resembles fine breadcrumbs. Stir in the sugar, then make a well in the centre. Add almost all the iced water and mix with a flat-bladed knife, using a cutting action, until the mixture comes together in beads. Add more water if the dough is too dry. Gather together and lift onto a lightly floured surface. Press into a ball and divide into two, making one half a little bigger. Cover with plastic wrap and refrigerate for 20 minutes.

- Preheat the oven to 200°C (400°F/Gas 6). Roll out the larger piece of pastry between two sheets of baking paper to line the base and side of the pie dish. Line the pie dish with the pastry and trim away any excess. Brush the base with marmalade and spoon the apple mixture into the shell. Roll out the remaining pastry between the baking paper until large enough to cover the pie. Brush water around the rim, then lay the pastry top over the pie. Trim off any excess pastry, pinch the edges and cut a few slits in the top to allow steam to escape.

- Re-roll the pastry scraps and cut into leaves for decoration. Lightly brush the top with egg, then sprinkle with sugar. Bake for 20 minutes, reduce the oven temperature to 180°C (350°F/Gas 4) and bake for another 15–20 minutes, or until golden.

LEMON ALMOND TART

preparation time 40 minutes
cooking time 1 hour
serves 6–8

LEMON PASTRY

250 g (9 oz/2 cups) plain (all-purpose) flour, sifted
55 g (2 oz/¼ cup) caster (superfine) sugar
125 g (4½ oz) chilled unsalted butter, softened
1 teaspoon finely grated lemon zest
2 egg yolks

FILLING

350 g (12 oz) ricotta cheese, sieved
80 g (2¾ oz/⅓ cup) caster (superfine) sugar
3 eggs, well beaten
1 tablespoon finely grated lemon zest
80 g (2¾ oz/½ cup) blanched almonds, finely chopped
30 g (1 oz/⅓ cup) flaked almonds
icing (confectioners') sugar, to dust (optional)

- Combine the flour, sugar and a pinch of salt in a large bowl. Make a well in the centre and add the butter, lemon zest and egg yolks. Work the flour into the centre with the fingertips of one hand until a smooth dough forms (add a little more flour if necessary). Cover in plastic wrap, flatten slightly, then refrigerate for 20 minutes.

- To make the filling, beat the ricotta and sugar together using electric beaters. Add the eggs gradually, beating well after each addition. Add the lemon zest, beating briefly to combine, and then stir in the chopped almonds.

• Preheat the oven to 180°C (350°F/Gas 4). Brush a 20 cm (8 inch) fluted loose-based flan (tart) tin with melted butter. Roll out the pastry on a lightly floured work surface large enough to line the tin. Line the tin with the pastry, trimming away the excess. Pour in the filling and smooth the top. Sprinkle with the flaked almonds and bake for 55–60 minutes, or until lightly golden and set.

• Allow to cool. Lightly dust with icing sugar, if desired, and serve at room temperature or chilled.

APPLE AND PEACH TURNOVERS

preparation time 20 minutes
cooking time 35 minutes
serves 4

40 g (1½ oz/⅓ cup) dried peaches, finely chopped
25 g (1 oz) unsalted butter
2 tablespoons soft brown sugar
3 granny smith apples, peeled, cored and finely chopped
1 teaspoon ground cinnamon
4 sheets frozen shortcrust pastry, thawed
1 egg, lightly beaten
sifted icing (confectioners') sugar, for dusting
2 tablespoons lightly toasted blanched almonds, finely chopped
1 tablespoon sweet sherry
2 tablespoons soft brown sugar
125 ml (4 fl oz/½ cup) thick (double/heavy) cream

- Preheat the oven to 180°C (350°F/Gas 4). Line a baking tray with baking paper.

- Put the dried peaches in a small bowl, pour 250 ml (9 fl oz/1 cup) boiling water over and leave to soak for 10 minutes.

- Put the butter and sugar in a frying pan and stir over medium heat until the butter melts. Add the apple and cinnamon and cook, stirring frequently, for 3–4 minutes, or until the apple has softened. Drain the soaked peaches, stir them through the apple mixture and set aside to cool.

- Lay the pastry sheets on a work surface and cut out eight circles using a 12 cm (4½ inch) cutter. Place 2 tablespoons of apple mixture in the middle of each circle. Lightly brush the edge of each pastry with beaten egg, then fold each one over to form a semi-circle, firmly pressing the edges to seal.

• Place the turnovers on the baking tray and brush the tops with the remaining egg. Bake for 25–30 minutes, or until the pastry is golden brown. Remove from the oven and allow to cool slightly before dusting with icing sugar.

• Combine the almonds, sherry, sugar and cream in a small bowl and serve with the warm turnovers.

FRUIT TART

preparation time 40 minutes
cooking time 40 minutes
serves 6

SHORTCRUST PASTRY

150 g (5½ oz/1¼ cups) plain (all-purpose) flour
2 tablespoons caster (superfine) sugar
90 g (3¼ oz) chilled unsalted butter, chopped
1 egg yolk
1 tablespoon iced water

FILLING

250 ml (9 fl oz/1 cup) milk
3 egg yolks
55 g (2 oz/¼ cup) caster (superfine) sugar
2 tablespoons plain (all-purpose) flour
1 teaspoon natural vanilla extract
strawberries, kiwi fruit and blueberries, to decorate
apricot jam, to glaze

- To make the pastry, sift the flour into a bowl and stir in the caster sugar. Using your fingertips, rub in the butter until the mixture resembles fine breadcrumbs. Make a well in the centre and add the egg yolk and iced water. Mix to a dough with a flat-bladed knife, using a cutting action. Turn out onto a lightly floured surface and gather together into a ball. Press together gently until smooth, and then roll out to fit a 10 x 34 cm (4 x 13½ inch) loose-based fluted flan (tart) tin. Line the tin with pastry and trim away any excess. Wrap in plastic wrap and refrigerate for 20 minutes. Preheat the oven to 190°C (375°F/Gas 5).

- Line the pastry-lined tin with baking paper and spread a layer of baking beads or uncooked rice evenly over the paper. Bake for 15 minutes, remove the paper and beads and bake for another 20 minutes, or until cooked on the base and golden brown around the edge. Set aside to cool completely.

• To make the filling, put the milk into a small saucepan and bring to the boil. Set aside while quickly whisking the egg yolks and sugar together in a bowl, until light and creamy. Whisk in the flour. Pour the hot milk slowly onto the egg mixture, whisking constantly. Wash out the pan, return the milk mixture to the pan and bring to the boil over medium heat, stirring with a wire whisk. Boil for 2 minutes, stirring occasionally. Transfer to a bowl, stir in the vanilla extract, and leave to cool, stirring frequently to avoid a skin forming. When cooled to room temperature, cover the surface with plastic wrap and refrigerate until cold.

• Cut the strawberries in half and peel and slice the kiwi fruit. Spoon the cold custard into the cold pastry shell, then arrange all the fruit over the custard, pressing in slightly. Heat the jam in the microwave or in a small saucepan until liquid, sieve to remove any lumps, then, using a pastry brush, glaze the fruit with the jam. Serve the tart on the same day, at room temperature. If it is to be left for a while on a hot day, refrigerate it.

Note *If you don't have a rectangular tin, this tart may be made in a 23 cm (9 inch) round flan tin. You can use different fruits to top the tart, according to taste and season.*

SWEET BAKED RICOTTA CAKE WITH CHERRIES

preparation time 20 minutes
cooking time 1 hour
serves 8–10

melted butter, for greasing
35 g (1¼ oz/⅓ cup) ground almonds
80 g (2¾ oz/⅓ cup) caster (superfine) sugar
1 kg (2 lb 4 oz/4 cups) firm, fresh ricotta cheese
1 teaspoon natural vanilla extract
½ teaspoon natural almond extract (optional)
finely grated rind of 1 orange
60 ml (2 fl oz/¼ cup) orange juice
4 eggs, lightly beaten
35 g (1¼ oz/¼ cup) plain (all-purpose) flour
125 g (4½ oz/1 cup) slivered almonds

STEWED CHERRIES

80 ml (2½ fl oz/⅓ cup) orange juice
90 g (3¼ oz/⅓ cup) caster (superfine) sugar
1 cinnamon stick
600 g (1 lb 5 oz) fresh or frozen pitted cherries

• Put all the ingredients for the stewed cherries in a saucepan. Cover with a lid, then slowly bring to the boil over medium heat. Cook for 8–10 minutes, or until the cherries are tender. Remove from the heat, cool to room temperature, then remove and discard the cinnamon stick.

• Meanwhile, preheat the oven to 170°C (325°F/Gas 3). Brush the base and side of a 23 cm (9 inch) springform tin with melted butter, then dust the tin with the ground almonds, turning the tin to coat it. Shake out any excess.

• Put the sugar, ricotta, vanilla and almond extracts, orange rind and orange juice in a food processor and blend until smooth, occasionally stopping the machine to scrape down the side. With the motor running, add the eggs, processing until smooth, then add the flour and process until just combined.

• Pour the mixture into the prepared tin, smoothing the top. Sprinkle with the slivered almonds and bake for 40–45 minutes, or until the cake is just firm in the middle. Turn the oven off, open the door slightly and leave the cake to cool completely. Serve at room temperature or chilled, with the stewed cherries spooned over.

PLUM AND POLENTA ROLY POLY

preparation time 20 minutes
cooking time 40 minutes
serves 4

60 g (2¼ oz/½ cup) raisins
75 g (2½ oz/½ cup) currants
315 g (11 oz/1 cup) plum jam
½ teaspoon ground cinnamon
1 teaspoon finely grated orange rind
225 g (8 oz/1½ cups) plain (all-purpose) flour
3 teaspoons baking powder
75 g (2½ oz/½ cup) polenta
75 g (2½ oz) unsalted butter, chopped
250 g (9 oz/1 cup) sour cream
sifted icing (confectioners') sugar, for dusting
custard, to serve
whipped cream, to serve
Cointreau or other orange-flavoured liqueur, to taste (optional)

• Preheat the oven to 180°C (350°F/Gas 4). Put the raisins, currants, jam, cinnamon and orange rind in a bowl and mix together well. Set aside.

• Sift the flour and baking powder into a bowl, then stir in the polenta. Using your fingertips, rub in the butter until the mixture resembles coarse breadcrumbs. Using a flat-bladed knife, stir in the sour cream until a rough dough forms, adding 1–2 tablespoons cold water if necessary.

• Roll the dough out on a floured surface into a rectangle measuring about 35 x 26 cm (14 x 10½ inches). Spread the jam and raisin mixture over the dough, leaving a 1.5 cm (⅝ inch) border around the edge. Brush the border with a little cold water.

• Starting with a longer edge, roll the dough up to form a 'log' about 35 cm (14 inches) long. Cut a sheet of baking paper a little longer than the roly poly, then carefully transfer the roly poly to the paper. Roll the log in the paper to enclose, leaving a little space for the roly poly to expand during baking. Twist both ends to close.

• Place the log on a baking tray and bake for 35–40 minutes, or until light golden and firm. Leave to cool for 5–10 minutes, then carefully unroll and remove the paper.

• Cut the roly poly into diagonal slices using a serrated knife. Dust generously with icing sugar and serve with custard and whipped cream. Stir a little liqueur into the custard, if desired.

JAFFA STEAMED PUDDING WITH CHOCOLATE SAUCE

preparation time 20 minutes
cooking time 40 minutes
serves 4

melted butter, for greasing
2 tablespoons marmalade
1 small orange
125 g (4½ oz) unsalted butter, softened
115 g (4 oz/½ cup) caster (superfine) sugar
75 g (2½ oz/½ cup) chopped dark chocolate, melted and cooled
2 eggs
110 g (3¾ oz/¾ cup) self-raising flour
35 g (1¼ oz/¼ cup) plain (all-purpose) flour
30 g (1 oz/¼ cup) unsweetened cocoa powder
60 ml (2 fl oz/¼ cup) milk

CHOCOLATE SAUCE

1 tablespoon soft brown sugar
125 g (4½ oz/¾ cup) chopped dark chocolate
80 ml (2½ fl oz/½ cup) cream
Cointreau or brandy, to taste (optional)

- Lightly brush a 1.25 litre (44 fl oz/5 cup) pudding basin with melted butter. Line the base with baking paper, then spread the marmalade over the base.

- Finely grate the orange rind and set aside. Using a sharp knife, remove all the white pith from the orange. Cut the orange into five or six slices widthways, removing any seeds. Overlap the slices around the bottom of the pudding basin and a little up the sides.

- Beat the butter, sugar and orange rind using electric beaters until light and fluffy. Add the melted chocolate and beat in well. Add the eggs one at a time, beating well after each addition.

• Sift together the flours and cocoa. Stir into the butter mixture in two batches, alternating with the milk. Spoon into the pudding basin and smooth the surface.

• Lay a sheet of foil on a work surface and top with a sheet of baking paper. Make a large pleat in the centre and place over the pudding basin, foil side up. Tie securely around the basin with string. Place on a trivet or an inverted heatproof saucer in a large saucepan. Fill the pan with boiling water to come halfway up the side of the basin. Bring the saucepan to the boil, then cover and cook over medium heat for 1 ½ hours, adding more water as necessary. Remove the string and foil cover and stand the pudding for 10 minutes to firm slightly.

• Put the chocolate sauce ingredients in a small saucepan and stir over low heat for 2–3 minutes, or until melted and glossy.

• Turn the hot pudding out onto a large plate. Cut into wedges and serve with the chocolate sauce. Stir some Cointreau or brandy into the chocolate sauce, if desired.

APRICOT SPONGE PUDDING

preparation time 20 minutes
cooking time 1 hour
serves 4

3 x 410 g (14½ oz) tins apricot halves in natural juice
55 g (2 oz/¼ cup) caster (superfine) sugar
125 g (4½ oz/⅔ cup) soft brown sugar
125 g (4½ oz) unsalted butter, softened
2 eggs
1 teaspoon natural vanilla extract
150 g (5½ oz/1 cup) plain (all-purpose) flour
2 teaspoons baking powder
60 ml (2 fl oz/¼ cup) milk
custard, to serve
2½ tablespoons amaretto (almond-flavoured liqueur)

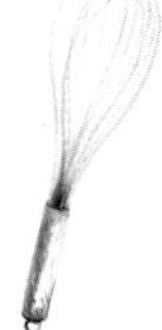

- Preheat the oven to 170°C (325°F/Gas 3). Put the apricots and their juice in a saucepan with the caster sugar over medium heat. Bring to the boil, then reduce the heat to medium–low and simmer for 5 minutes, or until the apricots have softened.

- Reserving the syrup in the pan, spoon the apricots into a 2 litre (70 fl oz/8 cup) baking dish (measuring about 14 x 20 x 7 cm/5½ x 8 x 2¾ inches). Place the syrup back over medium heat and simmer for a further 12–15 minutes, or until reduced by half. Pour over the apricots.

- Beat the brown sugar and butter with electric beaters until light and fluffy. Add the eggs one at a time, beating well after each addition. Stir in the vanilla. Sift the flour and baking powder together, then stir into the butter mixture alternately with the milk. Spoon the batter over the apricots.

- Bake for 30–35 minutes, or until the sponge is golden and firm to the touch. Sprinkle with the amaratto and serve hot, with custard.

FREE-FORM BLUEBERRY PIE

preparation time 20 minutes
cooking time 35 minutes
serves 4

185 g (6½ oz/1½ cups) plain (all-purpose) flour
60 g (2¼ oz/½ cup) icing (confectioners') sugar
125 g (4½ oz) chilled unsalted butter, cubed
60 ml (2 fl oz/¼ cup) lemon juice
500 g (1 lb 2 oz) blueberries
30 g (1 oz/¼ cup) icing (confectioners') sugar, extra
1 teaspoon finely grated lemon zest
½ teaspoon ground cinnamon
1 egg white, lightly beaten
icing (confectioners') sugar, extra, to dust
whipped cream or ice cream, to serve

- Preheat the oven to 180°C (350°F/Gas 4). Sift the flour and icing sugar into a bowl. Using your fingertips, rub in the butter until the mixture resembles fine breadcrumbs. Make a well in the centre and add almost all the lemon juice. Mix together with a flat-bladed knife, using a cutting action, until the mixture comes together in beads. Add the remaining lemon juice if the dough is too dry.

- Gently gather the dough together and lift onto a sheet of baking paper. Roll out to a circle about 30 cm (12 inches) in diameter. Cover with plastic wrap and refrigerate for 10 minutes. Put the blueberries in a bowl and sprinkle them with the icing sugar, lemon zest and cinnamon.

- Place the pastry (still on the baking paper) on a baking tray. Brush the centre of the pastry lightly with egg white. Pile the blueberry mixture onto the pastry in a 20 cm (8 inch) diameter circle, then fold the edges of the pastry over the filling, leaving the centre uncovered. Bake for 30–35 minutes. Dust with icing sugar and serve warm with whipped cream or ice cream.

CHOCOLATE BROWNIE ICE CREAM SANDWICHES

preparation time 20 minutes
cooking time 1 hour
serves 4

- 125 g (4½ oz) unsalted butter
- 250 g (9 oz/1⅔ cups) chopped good-quality dark chocolate
- 150 g (5½ oz/⅔ cup) caster (superfine) sugar
- 3 eggs, lightly beaten
- 2 teaspoons natural vanilla extract
- 100 g (3½ oz/⅔ cup) plain (all-purpose) flour
- 30 g (1 oz/¼ cup) unsweetened cocoa powder
- 65 g (2¼ oz/½ cup) sultanas (golden raisins)
- 4 individually wrapped ice cream slices
- 2 tablespoons icing (confectioners') sugar, sifted

• Preheat the oven to 170°C (325°F/Gas 3). Line a 20 x 30 cm (8 x 12 inch) rectangular tin with baking paper.

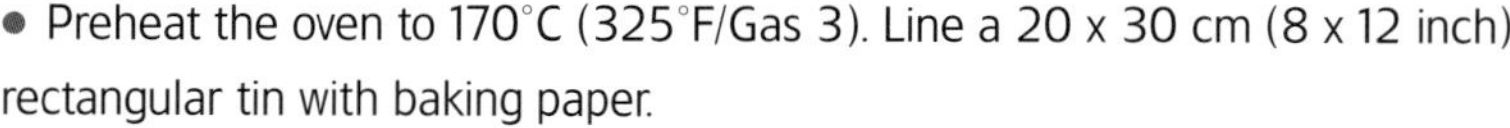

• Melt the butter in a small saucepan over low heat, then add the chocolate and stir until melted. Remove from the heat, add the sugar and stir well. Leave to cool slightly.

• Add the eggs one at a time to the chocolate mixture, mixing well after each addition. Stir in the vanilla.

• Sift the flour and cocoa into a bowl, then add the chocolate mixture and the sultanas and stir to combine. Pour the mixture into the baking tin, smoothing the top. Bake for 20–25 minutes, or until a cake tester inserted into the centre comes out clean. Leave the brownies in the tin to cool completely.

• To serve, cut the brownies into 6 x 9 cm (2½ x 3½ inch) portions, or into pieces the same size as the ice cream slices, trimming the edges. Place one brownie on each plate and top with an ice cream slice and another brownie. Dust with the icing sugar and serve.

MANGO-MERINGUE ROULADE

preparation time 20 minutes plus at least 1 hour 30 minutes chilling
cooking time 25 minutes
serves 6

5 egg whites, at room temperature
185 g (6½ oz/1 cup lightly packed) brown sugar
30 g (1 oz/¼ cup) ground hazelnuts

FILLING

250 ml (9 fl oz/1 cup) cream
425 g (15 oz) tinned mango, well drained
1 tablespoon icing (confectioners') sugar

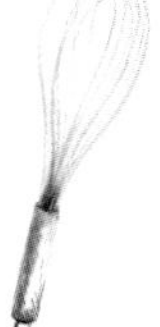

• Preheat the oven to 170°C (325°F/Gas 3). Grease a 24 x 34 cm (9½ x 13½ inch) tin and line with baking paper.

• Place the egg whites in a clean bowl and whisk with electric beaters until firm peaks form. Whisking constantly, slowly add the brown sugar, beating well after each addition, until the mixture is firm and glossy. Carefully fold in the hazelnuts using a large metal spoon. Spread the mixture evenly into the prepared tin. Bake for 8 minutes, then reduce the oven temperature to 150°C (300°F/Gas 2) and cook for 15 minutes, or until firm to the touch. Turn out onto a lightly greased sheet of baking paper. Remove the baking paper from the underside of the meringue. Cover the meringue with a clean tea towel (dish towel) and stand until cool.

• To make the filling, whisk the cream until firm peaks form. Combine the mango and icing sugar in a food processor and process until smooth. Gently fold half the mango purée into the cream. Spread over the cooled meringue and refrigerate the remaining mango purée. Starting from one long side of the meringue and using the paper as a guide, carefully roll the meringue to enclose the filling. Wrap in plastic wrap and refrigerate for 1½–2 hours, until ready to serve. Slice and serve drizzled with the remaining mango purée.

BREAD AND BUTTER PUDDING WITH RED WINE SAUCE

preparation time 20 minutes plus 30 minutes standing
cooking time 1 hour 30 minutes
serves 6

50 g (1¾ oz) unsalted butter, softened, plus extra, for greasing
300 g (10½ oz) day-old baguette, cut into 1.5 cm (⅝ inch) slices
5 eggs, lightly beaten
80 g (2¾ oz/⅓ cup) caster (superfine) sugar
375 ml (13 fl oz/1½ cups) milk
375 ml (13 fl oz/1½ cups) cream
40 g (1½ oz/⅓ cup) walnuts, roughly chopped

RED WINE SAUCE
500 ml (17 fl oz/2 cups) red wine
1 tablespoon caster (superfine) sugar
40 g (1½ oz/⅓ cup) sultanas (golden raisins)

• Preheat the oven to 160°C (315°F/Gas 2–3) and lightly grease a 1.5 litre (52 fl oz/6 cup) capacity, 23 x 14 cm (9 x 5½ inch) ovenproof dish. Lightly butter the baguette slices, then arrange them in layers in the dish. Combine the eggs, sugar, milk, cream and walnuts in a bowl and pour over the bread. Allow the pudding to stand for 15 minutes to absorb the liquid, then bake for 50–60 minutes, or until firm.

• To make the red wine sauce, combine the red wine, sugar and sultanas in a small saucepan over medium heat. Bring to the boil, then reduce the heat to medium–low and cook for 20–25 minutes, or until reduced and syrupy.

• Cool the pudding for 10–15 minutes, then serve with the red wine sauce drizzled over.

LEMON MERINGUE PIE

preparation time 1 hour
cooking time 45 minutes
serves 6

185 g (6½ oz/1½ cups) plain (all-purpose) flour
2 tablespoons icing (confectioners') sugar
125 g (4½ oz) chilled unsalted butter, chopped
60 ml (2 fl oz/¼ cup) iced water

FILLING AND TOPPING

30 g (1 oz/¼ cup) cornflour (cornstarch)
30 g (1 oz/¼ cup) plain (all-purpose) flour
230 g (8½ oz/1 cup) caster (superfine) sugar
185 ml (6 fl oz/¾ cup) lemon juice
3 teaspoons grated lemon zest
40 g (1½ oz) unsalted butter, chopped
6 eggs, separated
350 g (12 oz/1½ cups) caster (superfine) sugar, extra
½ teaspoon cornflour (cornstarch), extra

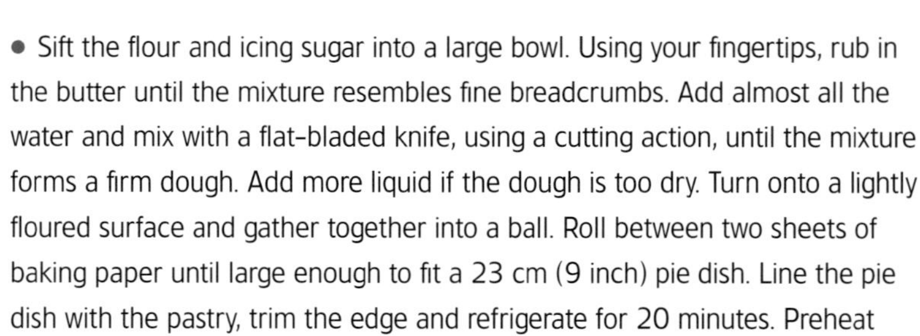

• Sift the flour and icing sugar into a large bowl. Using your fingertips, rub in the butter until the mixture resembles fine breadcrumbs. Add almost all the water and mix with a flat-bladed knife, using a cutting action, until the mixture forms a firm dough. Add more liquid if the dough is too dry. Turn onto a lightly floured surface and gather together into a ball. Roll between two sheets of baking paper until large enough to fit a 23 cm (9 inch) pie dish. Line the pie dish with the pastry, trim the edge and refrigerate for 20 minutes. Preheat the oven to 180°C (350°F/Gas 4).

• Line the pastry with a sheet of baking paper and spread a layer of baking beads or uncooked rice over the paper. Bake for 10 minutes, then remove the paper and beads and bake for a further 10 minutes, or until the pastry is lightly golden. Leave to cool.

• To make the filling, put the flours and sugar in a saucepan. Whisk in the lemon juice, zest and 375 ml (13 fl oz/1 ½ cups) water. Whisk continually over medium heat until the mixture boils and thickens. Reduce the heat and cook for 1 minute, then whisk in the butter and egg yolks, one egg yolk at a time. Transfer to a bowl, cover the surface with plastic wrap and cool completely.

• To make the topping, preheat the oven to 220°C (425°F/Gas 7). Beat the egg whites in a small dry bowl using electric beaters, until soft peaks form. Add the extra sugar gradually, beating until the meringue is thick and glossy. Beat in the extra cornflour. Pour the cold filling into the cold pastry shell and spread with meringue to cover, forming peaks. Bake for 5–10 minutes, or until lightly browned. Serve hot or cold.

APPLE TARTS WITH ROSEMARY SYRUP

preparation time 20 minutes
cooking time 45 minutes
serves 4

2 sheets frozen puff pastry, thawed
30 g (1 oz) unsalted butter, softened, plus 20 g (¾ oz) extra, cut into small cubes
2 tablespoons caster (superfine) sugar
1 teaspoon natural vanilla extract
1 teaspoon finely grated lemon rind
35 g (1¼ oz/⅓ cup) ground almonds
1 teaspoon plain (all-purpose) flour
2 small red apples (about 300 g/10½ oz)
50 ml (1½ fl oz) lemon juice

ROSEMARY SYRUP

55 g (2 oz/¼ cup) caster (superfine) sugar
8 small rosemary sprigs, leaves removed (about 2 tablespoons)

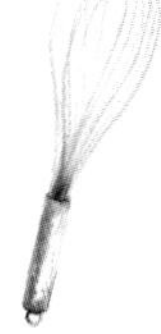

• Preheat the oven to 190°C (375°F/Gas 5) and line a large baking tray with baking paper. Lightly brush 1 pastry sheet with water and place the second sheet on top. Press together gently. Cut the pastry evenly into 4 squares and place on the tray. Knock up the pastry edges with the back of a dinner knife to help the pastry to rise and flake. Prick all over. Bake for 10 minutes until puffed and just golden. Remove from the oven and gently press down with a tea towel (dish towel) to remove any air pockets. Set aside to cool.

• Meanwhile, place 30 g (1 oz) butter, 1 tablespoon of the sugar, the vanilla and lemon rind in a small bowl and beat with a wooden spoon until creamy. Stir in the ground almonds and flour. Peel, quarter and core the apples. Put in a bowl and toss with the lemon juice.

- Spread the almond mixture over the pastry bases, leaving a 1 cm (½ inch) edge all around. Thinly slice the apples and arrange 2 sliced apple quarters on each pastry base, slightly overlapping the slices. Sprinkle each pastry with 1 teaspoon of the remaining caster sugar and dot with the extra butter. Bake for 20–25 minutes, or until the pastry is golden brown.

- Meanwhile, to make the rosemary syrup, combine 2 tablespoons water with the sugar in a small saucepan over a low heat. Stir to dissolve, then add the rosemary leaves and cook for 2–3 minutes, until the mixture becomes syrupy.

- Serve the tarts warm or at room temperature, drizzled with the syrup.

CARROT-APRICOT PUDDINGS WITH ORANGE CUSTARD

preparation time 20 minutes
cooking time 35 minutes
serves 6

60 g (2¼ oz/⅓ cup) finely chopped dried apricots
2 tablespoons apricot jam
2 eggs
125 ml (4 fl oz/½ cup) sunflower oil, plus extra, for greasing
95 g (3¼ oz/½ cup lightly packed) brown sugar
1 tablespoon golden syrup (dark corn syrup)
90 g (3¼ oz) carrot (about 1), peeled and finely grated
150 g (5½ oz/1 cup) plain (all-purpose) flour
3 teaspoons baking powder

ORANGE CUSTARD

375 ml (13 fl oz/1½ cups) purchased prepared custard
3 teaspoons finely grated orange rind
2 teaspoons orange juice or 1 teaspoon orange flower water

• To make the orange custard, combine the custard, orange rind and juice or flower water in a bowl and stir to combine well. Set aside.

• Preheat the oven to 180°C (350°F/Gas 4). Grease six 200 ml (7 fl oz) capacity ramekins or ovenproof moulds. Line the bases with baking paper.

• Put the apricots in a small bowl and pour over 2 tablespoons boiling water. Stand for 10 minutes, or until softened, then stir in the apricot jam. Divide the mixture among the ramekins.

• Combine the eggs, oil, brown sugar and syrup in a medium bowl and whisk using electric beaters until thick and pale. Gently stir in the carrot. Sift the flour and baking powder into a small bowl, then gently fold into the carrot mixture until combined.

• Divide the mixture among the ramekins, then tightly cover each with a piece of lightly oiled foil.

• Put the ramekins in a baking dish and pour in boiling water to come halfway up the sides of ramekins. Bake for 35 minutes, or until the puddings are golden and firm to the touch. Remove from the baking dish, take off the foil and cool slightly. Turn out onto serving plates and serve warm with the orange custard.

LEMON DELICIOUS WITH RASPBERRY CREAM

preparation time 20 minutes
cooking time 25 minutes
serves 6

50 g (1¾ oz) butter, melted, plus extra, for greasing
185 g (6½ oz) caster (superfine) sugar
1 teaspoon finely grated lemon rind
30 g (1 oz/¼ cup) self-raising flour, sifted
60 ml (2 fl oz/¼ cup) lemon juice
3 eggs, separated
310 ml (10¾ fl oz/1¼ cups) milk
250 ml (9 fl oz/1 cup) cream
1 tablespoon icing (confectioners') sugar, sifted
75 g (2½ oz/½ cup) frozen raspberries, thawed and crushed

- Preheat the oven to 180°C (350°F/Gas 4).

- Lightly grease six 250 ml (9 fl oz/1 cup) capacity ramekins or ovenproof cups. Combine 90 g (3¼ oz) of the caster sugar, lemon rind and flour in a bowl and mix well. In another bowl combine the lemon juice, melted butter, egg yolks and milk and whisk until smooth. Add the milk mixture to the flour mixture and mix until a batter is formed.

- Place the egg whites in a clean dry mixing bowl and whisk using electric beaters until soft peaks forms. Whisking continuously, slowly add the remaining sugar and whisk until firm peaks form. Add the meringue to the lemon mixture and fold gently until combined.

• Divide the mixture among ramekins or cups and place in a deep baking tray. Pour boiling water into the tray until it reaches a third of the way up the sides of the ramekins. Place in the oven carefully and bake for 25–30 minutes.

• Meanwhile, whisk the cream in a small bowl until thick, stir in the icing sugar and fold through the crushed raspberries.

• Serve the puddings topped with the raspberry cream.

CHOCOLATE STICKY DATE PUDDINGS WITH CARAMEL SAUCE

preparation time 20 minutes
cooking time 25 minutes
serves 6

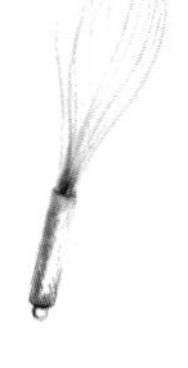

120 g (4¼ oz/¾ cup) chopped pitted dates
1½ teaspoons bicarbonate of soda (baking soda)
50 g (1¾ oz) unsalted butter, softened
60 g (2¼ oz/⅓ cup lightly packed) brown sugar
1 teaspoon natural vanilla extract
1 large egg
110 g (3¾ oz/¾ cup) self-raising flour
100 g (3½ oz/⅔ cup) chopped dark chocolate
thick (double/heavy) cream, to serve

CARAMEL SAUCE
140 g (5 oz/¾ cup lightly packed) brown sugar
200 ml (7 fl oz) cream
75 g (2½ oz) unsalted butter

- To make the caramel sauce, place the sugar, cream and butter into a small saucepan over low heat. Stir until the mixture is combined and the sugar has dissolved. Do not boil.

- Preheat the oven to 180°C (350°F/Gas 4) and lightly grease six 125 ml (4 fl oz/½ cup) ramekins. Place the dates and 185 ml (6 fl oz/¾ cup) water in a small saucepan over medium–high heat. Bring to the boil, then reduce the heat to medium–low and cook for 3 minutes. Remove from the heat, stir in the bicarbonate of soda and allow to cool.

- Beat the butter and sugar until pale and creamy. Add the vanilla and egg, beating well. Gently stir in the flour, chocolate and date mixture. Divide the mixture among the ramekins. Bake for 15 minutes, or until the puddings are risen and just firm to the touch; they will still be slightly sticky in the middle. Immediately run a knife around the side of each dish to loosen the puddings. Turn out onto serving plates.

- Drizzle the puddings with the caramel sauce and serve immediately with a dollop of cream.

PECAN PIE

preparation time 30 minutes
cooking time 1 hour 15 minutes
serves 6

SHORTCRUST PASTRY

185 g (6½ oz/1½ cups) plain (all-purpose) flour
125 g (4½ oz) chilled unsalted butter, chopped
2–3 tablespoons chilled water

FILLING

200 g (7 oz/2 cups) pecans
3 eggs, lightly beaten
50 g (1¾ oz) unsalted butter, melted and cooled
140 g (5 oz/¾ cup) soft brown sugar
170 ml (5½ fl oz/⅔ cup) light corn syrup
1 teaspoon natural vanilla extract

- Preheat the oven to 180°C (350°F/Gas 4). Sift the flour into a large bowl. Using your fingertips, rub the butter into the flour until the mixture resembles fine breadcrumbs. Add almost all the water and mix with a flat-bladed knife, using a cutting action, until the mixture comes together in beads. Add more water if the dough is too dry. Turn out onto a lightly floured work surface and gather together into a ball.

- Roll out the pastry to a 35 cm (14 inch) round. Line a 23 cm (9 inch) flan (tart) tin with pastry, trim the edges and refrigerate for 20 minutes. Pile the pastry trimmings together, roll out on baking paper to a rectangle about 2 mm (1/16 inch) thick, then refrigerate.

- Line the pastry-lined tin with a sheet of baking paper and spread a layer of baking beads or uncooked rice evenly over the paper. Bake for 15 minutes, remove the paper and beads and bake for another 15 minutes, until lightly golden. Cool completely.

- Spread the pecans over the pastry base. Whisk together the eggs, butter, sugar, corn syrup, vanilla extract and a pinch of salt until well combined, then pour over the nuts.

- Using a fluted pastry wheel or small sharp knife, cut narrow strips from half of the pastry trimmings. Cut out small stars with a biscuit (cookie) cutter from the remaining trimmings. Arrange decoratively over the filling. Bake the pie for 45 minutes, or until firm. Cool completely and serve at room temperature.

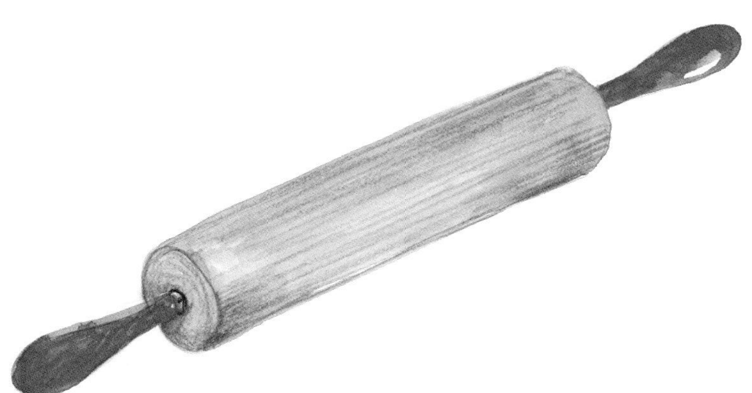

CHOCOLATE-CARAMEL TARTS

preparation time 20 minutes plus at least 2 hours chilling and 30 minutes standing
cooking time 35 minutes
serves 6

butter, for greasing
2 sheets frozen shortcrust (pie) pastry, thawed
1½ tablespoons caster (superfine) sugar

CARAMEL

230 g (8 oz/1 cup) caster (superfine) sugar
75 g (2½ oz) unsalted butter, chopped
80 ml (2½ fl oz/⅓ cup) cream

CHOCOLATE TOPPING

80 ml (2½ fl oz/⅓ cup) cream
150 g (5½ oz) dark chocolate (70% cocoa solids), chopped

• Preheat the oven to 180°C (350°F/Gas 4). Lightly grease six 10 cm (4 inch) wide, 2 cm (¾ inch) deep fluted tartlet tins. Sprinkle the pastry with the caster sugar. Using a 10 cm (4 inch) round cutter, cut out 6 rounds. Line each tin with a circle of pastry, pressing gently to cover the sides of the tins. Prick the bases with a fork. Place the tins in the freezer for 5 minutes. Line the pastry with baking paper, then pour in some baking beads or uncooked rice and bake for 10–12 minutes. Remove the paper and beads and bake for another 5 minutes, or until light golden. Cool.

• To make the caramel, combine 60 ml (2 fl oz/¼ cup) water and the sugar in a heavy-based saucepan over medium heat. Cook, without stirring, for 10–15 minutes, or until the mixture turns a medium caramel colour. Working quickly, remove the pan from the heat and add the butter and cream; take care as the mixture will spit. Swirl the pan to combine well, then divide the caramel among the cooled pastry cases. Refrigerate for at least 2 hours, or until the caramel has set.

• To make the topping, bring the cream to the boil in a small saucepan over medium heat. Add the chocolate, remove the pan from the heat and stir to combine well. Stand for 5 minutes, or until the chocolate has melted, then whisk the mixture until smooth. Cool slightly, then pour over the caramel in the pastry cases. Refrigerate until the chocolate has set. Remove from the refrigerator 30 minutes before serving.

BERRY PIE

preparation time 30 minutes
cooking time 45 minutes
serves 4–6

PASTRY

125 g (4½ oz/1 cup) self-raising flour
125 g (4½ oz/1 cup) plain (all-purpose) flour
125 g (4½ oz) chilled unsalted butter, chopped
2 tablespoons caster (superfine) sugar
1 egg, lightly beaten
60–80 ml (2–2½ fl oz/¼–⅓ cup) milk

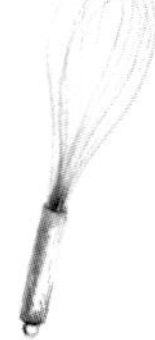

BERRY FILLING

2 tablespoons cornflour (cornstarch)
2–4 tablespoons caster (superfine) sugar, to taste
1 teaspoon grated orange zest
1 tablespoon orange juice
600 g (1 lb 5 oz) fresh berries (such as boysenberries, blackberries, loganberries, mulberries, raspberries or youngberries)

1 egg yolk, mixed with 1 teaspoon water, to glaze
icing (confectioners') sugar, to dust

• To make the pastry, sift the flours into a large bowl. Using your fingertips, rub in the butter until the mixture resembles fine breadcrumbs. Stir in the sugar, then add the egg and almost all the milk. Mix with a flat-bladed knife, using a cutting action, until the mixture comes together in beads. Add more milk if the dough is too dry. Turn out onto a lightly floured surface and gather into a ball. Divide into two portions and roll each portion out on a sheet of baking paper, ensuring one is the right size to cover a 750 ml (26 fl oz/3 cup) pie dish. Cover with plastic wrap and refrigerate for 30 minutes.

• To make the berry filling, mix the cornflour, caster sugar, orange zest and juice in a saucepan. Add half the berries to the pan and stir over low heat for 5 minutes, or until the mixture boils and thickens. Remove from the heat and set aside to cool. Add the remaining berries to the pan, pour into the pie dish and smooth the surface with the back of a spoon.

• Preheat the oven to 180°C (350°F/Gas 4). Place the pie top over the fruit and trim the edges. Make sure you do not stretch the pastry or it may shrink during baking and fall back into the dish. Using heart-shaped pastry cutters of various sizes, cut out enough hearts from the remaining pastry to cover the pie top. Arrange them on top of the pie, moistening each one with a little water to make it stick.

• Brush all over the surface with the egg glaze. Bake for 35–40 minutes, or until the pastry is crisp and golden brown. Dust with icing sugar just before serving. Serve the pie warm or cold.

Note *Use just one variety of berry or a combination if you prefer. If you want to make the pie when the berries are out of season, use frozen berries. Defrost the berries thoroughly, reserving the juice. Add the berries and juice to the filling and omit the orange juice. You can use tinned berries if you drain them well first.*

GINGERBREAD SOUFFLÉ

preparation time 30 minutes
cooking time 40 minutes
serves 6

120 g (4¼ oz) unsalted butter, plus extra for greasing
20 g (¾ oz) caster (superfine) sugar, for dusting soufflé cups
100 g (3½ oz/⅔ cup) plain (all-purpose) flour
125 ml (4 fl oz/½ cup) milk
125 ml (4 fl oz/½ cup) cream
5 large eggs, separated
280 g (10 oz/1½ cups lightly packed) brown sugar
1 tablespoon ground ginger
1 teaspoon cinnamon
300 g (10½ oz) thick (double/heavy) cream
2 tablespoons brandy
2 teaspoons icing (confectioners') sugar, for dusting

• Preheat the oven to 200°C (400°F/Gas 6). Lightly grease six 250 ml (9 fl oz/1 cup) capacity ramekins. Pour a little caster sugar into each, swirling to coat the inside of the ramekins and shaking out the excess. Place the ramekins on a baking paper-lined baking tray and set aside.

• Melt the butter in a saucepan over medium heat, add the flour, stirring to combine well, then cook, stirring constantly, for 1 minute. Combine the milk and cream in a jug and gradually stir into the flour mixture. Stirring constantly to prevent lumps forming, cook for 3–4 minutes or until the mixture thickens. Transfer the mixture to a large bowl and whisk in the egg yolks, one at a time.

• Combine the brown sugar with the spices and gradually whisk into the egg mixture until smooth. Set aside.

• Beat the egg whites until firm peaks form, then stir a third of the egg whites into the milk mixture to loosen it a little. Then, very gently and gradually, fold the remaining egg whites into the milk mixture.

• Reduce the oven temperature to 180°C (350°F/Gas 4). Divide the soufflé mixture among the ramekins and run your finger along the inside of each one to create a small ridge. Bake for 30–35 minutes, or until the soufflés have risen above the dish.

• Meanwhile, combine the cream and brandy in a small bowl and whisk until soft peaks form.

• Dust the soufflés with the icing sugar and serve immediately, with the brandy cream on the side.

VANILLA RICE TART WITH APRICOT PURÉE

preparation time 50 minutes plus 50 minutes chilling time
cooking time 1 hour 20 minutes
serves 6–8

80 g (2¾ oz) cold butter, chopped, plus extra for greasing
225 g (8 oz/1½ cups) plain (all-purpose) flour
30 g (1 oz/¼ cup) icing (confectioners') sugar, plus extra, for dusting
1 egg yolk

VANILLA RICE FILLING

110 g (3¾ oz/½ cup) short-grain rice
250 ml (9 fl oz/1 cup) milk
300 ml (10½ fl oz/1¼ cups) cream
60 g (2¼ oz/¼ cup) caster (superfine) sugar
1 teaspoon natural vanilla extract
2 egg yolks
100 g (3½ oz) ricotta cheese

APRICOT PURÉE

100 g (3½ oz/¾ cup) dried apricots, chopped
1½ tablespoons caster (superfine) sugar
¼ teaspoon ground cinnamon

• Grease a shallow 22 cm (8½ inch) round fluted flan tin with a removable base. Place the flour, butter and sugar in a food processor and process until the mixture resembles breadcrumbs. Add the egg yolk and about 1 tablespoon of iced water, then using the pulse button, briefly process until the mixture just comes together. Turn onto a lightly floured surface and gather into a ball. Wrap in plastic wrap and refrigerate for 20 minutes.

• Roll the pastry between 2 sheets of baking paper lightly dusted with flour until it is large enough to line the base and side of the tin. Remove the baking paper, lift the pastry into the tin, easing it in to fit, then trim off any excess. Prick the base with a fork. Line with baking paper and fill with baking beads or rice. Refrigerate for 30 minutes. Preheat the oven to 180°C (350°F/Gas 4). Bake the pastry shell for 10 minutes. Remove the beads and paper and bake for another 10 minutes, or until dry and light golden.

• To make the vanilla rice filling, combine the rice, milk and 125 ml (4 fl oz/ ½ cup) of the cream in a saucepan. Stir over medium heat until the mixture comes to the boil. Reduce heat to low, cover and cook for about 15 minutes, stirring occasionally, until the rice is nearly tender and the mixture is thick. Remove from the heat, stir in the sugar and vanilla, then cool. Stir in the egg yolks, ricotta and remaining cream. Pour the rice mixture into the prepared pastry case. Bake for 30–35 minutes, or until the mixture is just set.

• To make the apricot purée, combine the apricots, 175 ml (5½ fl oz/¾ cup) water, the sugar and cinnamon in a small saucepan and bring to the boil over medium heat. Reduce the heat to low and cook for 5 minutes, or until soft. Remove from the heat and allow to cool. Process until smooth. If the mixture is very thick, add a little extra water.

• Remove the tart from the oven and cool to room temperature. Dust with icing sugar and serve in wedges with the apricot purée.

PASSIONFRUIT TART

preparation time 30 minutes
cooking time 1 hour
serves 8

- 90 g (3¼ oz/¾ cup) plain (all-purpose) flour
- 2 tablespoons icing (confectioners') sugar
- 2 tablespoons custard powder or instant vanilla pudding mix
- 30 g (1 oz) unsalted butter
- 60 ml (2 fl oz/¼ cup) light evaporated milk
- icing (confectioners') sugar, extra, to dust

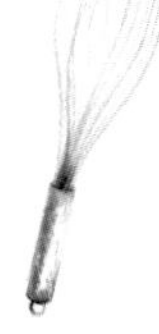

FILLING

- pulp from about 8 passionfruit
- 125 g (4½ oz/½ cup) ricotta cheese
- 1 teaspoon natural vanilla extract
- 30 g (1 oz/¼ cup) icing (confectioners') sugar
- 2 eggs, lightly beaten
- 185 ml (6 fl oz/¾ cup) light evaporated milk

• Preheat the oven to 200°C (400°F/Gas 6). Lightly spray a 23 cm (9 inch) loose-based flan (tart) tin with oil spray. Sift the flour, icing sugar and custard powder into a bowl. Using your fingertips, rub in the butter until the mixture resembles fine breadcrumbs. Add almost all the milk. Mix with a flat-bladed knife, using a cutting action, until the mixture forms a soft dough. Add more milk if the dough is too dry. Bring together on a lightly floured work surface until just smooth. Form into a ball, wrap in plastic wrap and refrigerate for 15 minutes.

• Roll the pastry out on a lightly floured surface, large enough to fit the tin, then refrigerate for 15 minutes. Cover with baking paper and fill with baking beads or uncooked rice. Bake for 10 minutes, remove the paper and beads and bake for another 5–8 minutes, or until golden. Cool. Reduce the oven to 160°C (315°F/Gas 2–3).

• Strain the passionfruit pulp to remove the seeds, reserving 2 teaspoons of seeds. Beat the ricotta with the vanilla extract and icing sugar until smooth. Add the eggs and passionfruit pulp, reserved passionfruit seeds and milk, then beat well. Put the tin on a baking tray and gently pour in the mixture. Bake for 40 minutes, or until set. Cool in the tin. Dust the edges with icing sugar just before serving.

Index

Q

R

Tunisian brik 95